From Zero to Published

How to Sell Your First Book Without an Email List or a Budget

Jason Hamilton

Myth HQ, LLC

Contents

Introduction

Hello there! (he says in his Obi-Wan Kenobi voice) I'm so very glad that you've picked up this book. Why? Because it means you want to be an author.

I've been planning on writing this one for a long while now, ever since I began preparing to launch my very first series. Those were stressful times, and there are a lot of things I know now that I wish I had known then. But there were also a number of things that worked really well when I finally did launch. Hopefully I'll be able to impart some of that knowledge on to you.

Who Is This Book For?

I've written this book to be of use to those looking to publish their own book for the first time. That's for those who are looking to self-publish (or indie-publish as we often prefer to say).

This is *not* a book for those seeking the traditional publishing route. This book will not teach you how to send query letters, find an agent, and eventually give your book to someone else to publish it for you. There are plenty of other resources on that subject (my best suggestion would be *How to Publish Your Book*, by Jane Friedman through The Great Courses. It's fantastic.)

No, this book is for those who want to break away from the blood and tears of the traditionally published world and venture out on their own adventure. But it's dangerous to go alone, so take this advice with you.

Now, I will say that I am a writer of fantasy. Most of my interests are in fantasy or science fiction. However, I've tried to structure this book so it will be useful to writers of all genres. That being said, not every marketing strategy will work for all audiences. Children's books and middle-grade, for example, involve wildly different marketing strategies. But most of the principles in this book will work for fantasy, science fiction, thriller/suspense/horror, and even romance. But just know that you may have to tweak a number of things to make it work even better in your niche.

Anyway, if you fit the above description, this book is for you. If you're looking to make it on your own, to have a guarantee of getting your book visible for readers, not to mention full control over your own work, then read on!

Who am I?

My name is Jason Hamilton. I'm an independently published author. I understand some people like to know a little bit about the authors of the books they're reading. So here it goes, I guess.

I wouldn't say I'm that guy who has been writing since they were capable of holding a pen up straight. Yes, I have always been into storytelling, and yes, some of that involved writing. I was a very creative child growing up. But much of my attention was turned towards filmmaking. I made my first small film around the age of 12. The writing was a part of that, of course, but I was equally fascinated with the process of filming, editing, and creating visual effects for those films.

Looking back, that last part was the more impressive. I learned how to make convincing-looking lightsabers on film. And at age 14, I completed my first proper Star Wars fan film. It was 24 minutes long, not bad for a 14 year old. Basically I was that nerd in high school that all of you probably knew about, but never interacted with.

That was the first time I actually began to study the art of storytelling. I remember picking up a lot of books about the topic, learning the basics of story structure and applying them to my next film, a sequel to the first. It was 45 minutes long, and a significant improvement on the first, though I still wouldn't let you see it if you asked.

I was thoroughly engrossed in the subject by this time, even going so far as to read huge biographies of people such as Stephen Spielberg and George Lucas, two of my idols. Seriously, what teenager reads 400-page biographies of anyone?

I did.

But then I went to college, applied to film school...and was rejected. But that wouldn't stop me!!! I applied again...and was rejected again. This time, I was not be allowed to apply a third time. I was devastated. It seemed my entire world, my entire plan for the future had been dashed to pieces. I spent the next few semesters trying to figure out what I would do next. I honestly had no idea. All my plans had been fixed on film school. In the end, I went with what I thought was similar enough, and easy to get through, as I had wasted a lot of my time at college up to this point. That backup plan was an English degree.

My English degree is where I learned the basics of writing. Not just writing fiction (believe it or not, fiction writing was only a teeny-tiny sliver of an English degree), but paragraph structure, persuasive writing, and much more. I began to see that there was a lot more to this writing thing than I had previously thought.

Despite all this, I didn't write much fiction other than the occasional short story. Because, you see, I had this one little problem that kept holding me back: I knew that publishing was hard to manage, and that very few people who tried ever achieved it. And given my recent double rejection from film school, I wasn't eager for more. Furthermore, I knew that many people who *did* get published never really made a living with that writing. And it simply wasn't worth it to me to go through all that effort only to be rejected or even be accepted but not make a living anyway.

So I never really thought of writing as a career. Instead, I got into content marketing after graduating, and learned HTML, CSS, and Wordpress so I could create websites, which is still one of my favorite hobbies today. I make all of my own websites (and no, I'm not for hire, sorry).

Those skills would serve me well, because they are what eventually got me my job working at Kindlepreneur, but I'll get to that.

Side note: learning how to build and develop content for a website is still one of the best ways to apply an English degree, in my opinion.

Anyway, what does all this have to do with publishing? Well, this entire experience gave me a background in a number of areas that have become invaluable to my career as an author. From my early days as a "filmmaker" I gained my first introduction to storytelling. From my English degree, I gained a knowledge of how to write well. And from my career after earning my degree, I learned how to market something online. This last part was especially important.

It wasn't until after college that I discovered the self-publishing industry. It was around 2016 or so that I picked up a massive fantasy volume that was super popular and selling like hotcakes on Audible. I took a listen, and thought it was very good. When I investigated further, I discovered that it hadn't gone through a traditional publisher, but was (gasp) published by the author directly!

Somehow I had lived through the entire Kindle revolution without realizing that it was possible for books to be self-published, many of them actually good! I think I carried much of the bias that many uninformed people have that self-publishing was an avenue for those who couldn't get published traditionally, and therefore was subpar to what you'd find in the stores. Oh, how wrong I was.

As I researched the topic further, I discovered that most of the indie authors out there never even wanted to go the traditional route. These were people who knew their audiences just as well, if not better than the big publishing houses. These were people who wanted more money per book sold. These were people with marketing experience like myself. These were people who wanted full control over their work.

They were people like me.

I read a few books on the subject, but it wasn't until I picked up Chris Fox's *5000 Words Per Hour* that my eyes truly opened for the first time (seriously, go read that book). I began to realize that many of the lies told to me concerning publishing (like the fact that you can only publish 1-2 books a year) were straight up poppycock. I could do so much more!

Side note: this is especially true now that AI is a thing, although to keep the quality high, it still takes time, but far less than most authors think.

Now it's worth noting that, although I had never written any of them down, I had a ton of book ideas in my head at this point, probably enough to write over a hundred books. I had almost resigned myself to the fact that I would never seen them actually realized. Once again, oh how wrong I was.

As I learned more about the industry, I became truly motivated for the first time to write my first book. So naturally I didn't write it as a book, I wrote it as a serial, thinking I was being innovative and clever by trying something new.

Pro tip: do not try to be innovative when you're just starting out. You won't even know how to be innovative until you've worked long and hard doing things the way everyone else does them. Then you'll know enough to be innovative.

Needless to say, that serial got no traction whatsoever. But that didn't stop me. I began writing my first proper book in 2017. I finished it in 2018, and wrote the second and third book within a few months after that. In August of 2018, I released all three books, and applied every single marketing and release strategy I'd been learning for the two or so years up to that point.

I sold nearly 1000 copies of my books in that first month alone, and since then, that one series has gone on to make a consistent three figures every month. Now this might sound disappointing to some of you, who may have expected me to say that my series sold like gangbusters and I'm now living on a private island in the Caribbean sipping a Piña Colada while my butler transcribes these very words as I say them. Believe me, I'm disappointed that's not the case as well.

But what you'll find as you read this book is that starting off as an author is not an easy challenge. Many write upwards of twenty books without even seeing three figures in monthly sales. I'm honestly thrilled at what I've managed to achieve so far. I eventually released more series, and they've done about as well as the first.

How This Book is Structured

So...allow me to show you how I had the success I've had with self-publishing so far, especially on my first series. I'll share the tips and strategies that led to my selling 1000 books in the first month, as well as some strategies I wish I had used in that initial book launch.

I've divided this book into five steps, showing you exactly the route that I would take if I were starting over again to gain maximum effectiveness on a first-time book or series. These steps are:

- Step 1: The Reader Magnet

- Step 2: The Newsletter

- Step 3: The Books

- Step 4: Self-publishing

- Step 5: The Marketing

It is my goal to become a full-time writer, and despite the fact that self-publishing has become an increasingly crowded space, it is still, by far, the best way to make a living as a writer. Only a very lucky few ever make a living by going the traditional route, even when published. But in indie publishing, there are hundreds of writers making six-figure incomes, and there are likely to be more. Readers are increasing, and so are the methods of reaching those readers. So even though the world of self-publishing is a little more difficult to break into than it was a few years ago, there has still never been a better time to be a writer. I aim for this book to give you the highest chance possible of breaking into that space.

So, let's get started...

FREE BONUS!

By purchasing this book, you can gain access to my "AI Foundations Course" which walks you through exactly what you need to do in order to incorporate AI into your writing (should you want to), and to do it in such a way that keeps you in the creative position, rather than letting the AI do all the work for you.

Becoming an author in today's age means embracing technology, and that course will give you everything you need to know.

As an added bonus, you'll receive "The Plot Module Cheat Sheet" - a guide to crafting the perfect plot, chapter by chapter (which I talk about later in this book).

You can get these by signing up for my free community at https://nerdynovelist.com/free or using the QR code below.

The 80/20 Rule

Before we dive into the individual steps, I can't go much further without talking briefly about the 80/20 rule, also known as the Pareto Principle, after the man who first identified the phenomenon.

The basic idea behind the 80/20 rule is that most of your success will come from only a small subsection of the things you actually do. In other words, 20% of your work will result in 80% of your success.

I have personally found this to be true. There are a lot of things I've done in the past that seemed important at the time, and may even have resulted in some success that I would not have seen otherwise, but ultimately were a waste of time. Instead, I could have focused on those tasks that I was spending less time on, but were resulting in the bulk of my success. The more you focus on those high-return tasks, the more results you will achieve.

And that's what I want for you: results.

This advice is never more important than when you're just starting out. You cannot afford to waste a lot of time on fruitless marketing strategies. You need to focus all of your attention on the tasks that matter most. And that is the primary purpose of this book: to sort out the wheat from the chaff and help you identify what you should be working on TODAY!

I'll go into some of these in detail throughout the book, and even touch on a couple of other tasks that many authors do, but might not have outstanding results and therefore might be something you don't need to focus on so early in your career. Instead, focus on the 20% wok that gets 80% of the results. Some of the tasks that produce those results include:

- Outlining

- Write. Write. Write.

- Book Covers

- Newsletters

- Self-improvement

- Advertising (maybe)

Notice that I didn't mention some things you might expect like social media or editing on there. That doesn't mean they're not important, but sometimes we *can* get a little too caught up in them that we neglect other, more important tasks. And you'll also notice that all but two of those things can be done without spending a dime. Self-publishing does not have to break your bank to work, and neither should it consume all of your waking moments. Writing should be fun, and it's not fun when it costs an arm and a leg that you never get back.

That said, the book market is such today that you *do* need to spend some money if you want to succeed. But placing your money in the wrong bucket could result in throwing it out the window. You want to spend money on the things that will actually get results. And you want to make sure your books are set up properly so they're worth spending money on. You can have the best advertising campaign in the world, but if your book isn't properly set up (with a good cover and blurb) than you will not see any results.

So spending money, just like spending time, also uses the 80/20 rule. You only want to spend money on those things that produce 80% of the results. If you can do that, spending both your time and hard-earned pennies on the things that matter most, you will be well on your way to a successful launch of your first book.

Choosing What to Write

I start here, because if you choose the wrong thing to write, it can completely kill any chance you have of successfully launching your book. I found this out the hard way when I tried to write my first serial and published it on my website.

I thought I was being so clever when I wrote it. The story was part urban fantasy, part science fiction, part time travel, and part superhero. My logic was that it would appeal to everyone! Yeah...

Pro tip: If you try to appeal to everyone, you will appeal to no one.

That book was incredibly difficult to market. I didn't even know what I was doing when I tried to develop the book cover. I had this nifty idea of making it look like an unfinished comic book. I thought I was being so original and clever. The end result is that the book cover didn't look anything like any genre, and therefore only people who already knew me picked it up.

If you don't get anything else out of this book, please understand this: if your book is not familiar to pre-established audiences, you will never sell a single copy to anyone but your grandmother. This not only means the story should be familiar to an audience, but also your book cover and your book blurb.

This is known among publishing circles as "Writing to Market"....

Yes, You Should Write to Market

I've already told you about my first attempt at a full-length project: my serial. It was all over the place in terms of my target market. These days I'm actually planning on re-writing it, but rather than be the superhero-time-travel-urban-fantasy-science-fiction-thriller melting pot that it was, I'm going to focus on this one as an Urban Fantasy.

The good news is that I actually won't have to change much. I'm tweaking the main character's back story from being an English teacher to being a cop (a common trope in Urban Fantasy), and I'm shifting certain elements of the plot to be a little less superhero, and a little more fantasy. Thankfully, the two aren't that different from each other! Superheroes have monsters, so do urban fantasies. Superheroes have over-the-top action, so do a lot of urban fantasies.

The lesson here is this: you don't have to change your story very much to make it fit an established genre. Look, I know your book is your baby, and adhering to genre "tropes" might feel a little like bastardizing it. How dare I even suggest that you take your precious, original story and make it less precious and less original.

But chances are, you already have some story ideas that pretty much fit the genre already. If you were to draw a Venn diagram of all the story ideas in your brain, with all the different genres out there, I bet you would find several that overlap. In fact, most of them will likely fit, even if some require some light tweaking.

Objections to writing to market usually come in two varieties:

1. Writing to market is unoriginal and I want to stand out. People won't want to read the same old story over again.

2. I prefer to write by the seat of my pants (pantsers) and I can't be creatively tied down by tropes.

Let's address each of these in turn.

Concern #1: Writing to Market is Not Original.

From one very limited view, this is somewhat true. Writing to market does involve identifying a lot of tropes and using those tropes over again in your story. Put that way, it almost sounds like stealing. Why would anyone do such a thing like that!?

One word: Resonance.

People say they want original stories, but they actually don't. The top movies at the box office are always those that are part of some mega-series that people are already familiar with, or at least adhere to a number of mega-action-movie tropes. The truly original films usually do not make a lot of money. Hollywood hasn't run out of original ideas. We aren't buying tickets to the ones that *are* original.

The truth is, we don't want something foreign, we crave the familiar. This is widely true for humanity across the board, independent of culture, nationality, race, religion, orientation, etc. It's a part of who we are. This is also very true of how we read books.

What people really mean when they say they want something original, is that they want the familiar but slightly different. Putting a unique twist on familiar tropes is often highly successful. That is what will resonate with people. Tolkien drew on common medieval myths for Lord of the Rings, George Lucas studied Joseph Campbell's research on the monomyth (a story structure found throughout history) and used that as the basis for Star Wars. J.K. Rowling did much of the same thing when writing Harry Potter. Pretty much every mega-phenomenon in storytelling has its roots in something already familiar. But in most cases, each one had a unique spin on it.

If your book does not resonate with the right reader, it will not sell. Period. The same is true of your marketing. If that does not ALSO resonate with the right reader, you will not sell. I will come back to this concept several times through-out this book.

Now, the second part to this concern is that by writing to market, you won't stand out. It's true that it's sometimes hard to stand out from the crowd. But here's the thing, this is your first book. You're not necessarily going to know how to stand out when you still don't know how to fit in. You must become a slave to the rules of the genre, to the letter of the law, before you will become familiar enough to know when and how to break those rules in a way that will wow your audience.

That is why I usually recommend to anyone just starting out that they play it safe. Because, and I'm being honest here, it's not likely that your very first series will sell very many copies. And honestly, once you're more experienced and look back on your first book, you might be glad it didn't. Surprises and exceptions have been known to happen, but I want you to go into this experience with the idea that you may fail.

BUT PLEASE DON'T THROW AWAY THE BOOK JUST YET!

What I should also point out is that failing is the most im-portant step to success. Yes, it can be difficult to have instant, quit-my-job levels of success on a first book or series. But it is much MORE likely that you can have those results with your second or third. And you will never get there without writing your first series.

So back to playing it safe. We've been conditioned for a long time that our breakout book has to be something incredible, some ridiculously good hook or a twist ending that just blows everybody's mind. This is due, largely, to the fact that for traditional publishing to happen, this is generally true. They want to publish the cream of the crop, which is why so many people get rejection letter after rejection letter. So we naturally assume that our first book has got to be our best.

Whatever you do, do not do this! (that's a lot of "dos")

I've got one other piece of bad news for you. Your first book will not be all that good.

WAIT NO, PLEASE DON'T THROW ME AWAY!

Once again, I say this simply because you're at the beginning of your game. You will improve dramatically with each book you write, that's simply the way it is. I cringe when I look back on books I wrote just a few months ago. I'm that much better. I'm sure one day I will look back at this book and consider pulling it off the market because it's so bad (by my future-me standards). I can already guarantee that it will need to be updated at some point (*future me's note: it was*). But regardless, your first book is not going to be your best, because you *will* get better with each one.

So once again, let me emphasize, I believe you should play it safe when you write your first book.

In addition to my hodgepodge of a serial, I also had a book I was writing that I was super excited about. It was based on Shakespeare's Hamlet, but with what I thought was a pretty cool twist. Thankfully, as I was writing it, I read a number of books like this one. While reading those books, I realized that the story I was writing did not really match any particular genre. I didn't even know what category to put it under on Amazon.

So I did one of the hardest things I'd done up to that point. I abandoned it at around 20K words. Instead, I picked a series I had tucked away for some later date that better fit genre conventions. It was a more traditional high fantasy that was really more of background information on another series I hoped to do later. I knew if I wrote it, I could fit it into an existing market. I also knew that if it wasn't that great, I wouldn't be too crestfallen because it wasn't my *pièce de résistance*. It was one that I could allow to fail, and this is a very important tip I give people, that not many other authors will give. It's okay for your first series to fail. When you can give yourself permission for that to happen, a lot of doors will open up for you.

Concern #2: Pantsers and Creative Restriction

"Pantsers" is a common term for those who do not outline their book and instead write by the seat of their pants, just making up the story as they go along. This is in contrast to outliners who...outline.

Now, there have been endless debates on which one is better, pantsing or outlining. The truth is, neither one is better or worse.

HOWEVER!

This is self-publishing. It's a slightly different industry. You see, pantsing has a habit of really REALLY slowing you down. Because inevitably as you're writing the story, you will write yourself into a corner and will have to go back and re-write whole sections. Or you'll discover that you need to add a completely new character into the book. Or the setback could be due to any number of reasons. Many of these problems can be avoided with a solid outline (which in my view is just pantsing ahead of time before you write).

Because pantsing is typically much slower, which means you'll be able to produce less in a year, which will mean fewer books, which will mean fewer sales. Libbie Hawker in her phenomenal book about outlining, *Take Off Your Pants!* talks about this specifically at the start of the book. Yes, there's no better or worse way to write a book. But outlining *is* better if you want a good chance of making a living with your books

So to address this concern, yes, writing to market and outlining can interfere with pantsing. But if you want the best chance to make a career of this (and it's totally fine if you don't), then you should outline.

Now I know there are probably many of you who will insist on not writing to market. And to you, I say, good luck. And I'm not saying that sarcastically. I really mean it. There are, of course, people out there who have been successful at it. They're rare, and many of them had experience that you don't. But that doesn't mean it's impossible. Just remember, it's unlikely. If you do have a completely original masterpiece that you want to write, by all means go ahead and write it. My only suggestion would be to wait, just wait until you have a more established audience. Then you will be able to take a risk like writing an experimental book.

Step 1: The Reader Magnet

1

NEWSLETTERS AND THE READER MAGNET

Alright, so by now I'm assuming you have an idea of what you want to write for your next book, HOWEVER, we're not going to talk about that just yet. First, I want to talk about one thing that we want to set up first: your email newsletter.

Email is one of the oldest forms of digital marketing in the book, and it is still one of the best (if not *the* best). It's so important, that I actually have my students set up their newsletter *before* they even finish their book.

Just like we all still have mailboxes for snail mail, most of us still have an email. While there are certainly other ways to interact with readers online, most of those require email as well. As such, I'm pretty sure that email is never going away, at least not in our lifetime.

This is actually a very good thing, considering the rapid change inherent in the digital world. Having an email list creates a sort of solidarity that we don't get with social media or other ways to connect to readers. It's more permanent, relatively speaking. It's also a form of owned media.

What do I mean by "owned media"? Well, let me give you an example. It used to be that Facebook pages were the bomb. If you had a large following on your Facebook page, all you had to do was post, and every single person who liked that page would get your post in their newsfeed. But one day, Facebook changed their algorithm, and all of that changed. Now, very few will see your post naturally. For the rest, you have to pay Facebook to show it to them. It was annoying at the time, but there was nothing anyone could do about it.

That is not the case with your email list. Sure, you might use an email provider to distribute your emails, and those companies will fluctuate as well. But in most cases, you own the email list. You can download it and migrate to another email service if need be, but you will always be able to contact those people as long as they decide to remain subscribed.

Imagine an email list of ten thousand dedicated readers, all of them just waiting for your next book to drop. When you finally release your book, all you have to do is send it out to your subscribers, then sit back and watch the money roll in.

Okay, it's not always that simple, but that is the concept behind an email list. They are your subscribers, not Facebook's, not Twitter's, yours.

The bad news is that most people are constantly inundated with dozens, often hundreds of emails a day, so it can be difficult to stand out from the crowd at times, and you're more likely to see unsubscribes from people who are no longer interested. But that's okay! Email is still probably the most viable way to get your book out to the right readers.

But let's say you don't have an email list set up as a first-time author. How do you go about creating one, and how can you gain subscribers if you don't even have a book out yet?

This is exactly one of the questions that I had when I was just starting out as an author. I knew I had this book I wanted to launch, and I wanted to get it out to as many of the right readers as possible, but the problem was...I didn't have a book out. I couldn't get subscribers without a book, but I couldn't sell the book without more subscribers. It was a Catch 22.

Fortunately, there are ways to get around this, and that leads us to discuss reader magnets.

The Reader Magnet

A reader magnet is a fancy name for some kind of freebie that you give away to subscribers on your email list. It's called a reader magnet because it is meant to attract readers of your genre to subscribe to your list in order to get what you have available.

It will be difficult, if not impossible, to get anyone to subscribe to your email list without a reader magnet, especially when you're just starting out.

But what does a reader magnet look like?

It can take multiple forms. The most common are prequel short stories, inter-quel short stories (taking place alongside or between books in your series), deleted scenes, special epilogues, the same scenes from your book from a different character's perspective, or even whole books.

Remember that serial I wrote that was all over the place? Well I now include that for free on my newsletter. I write at least one reader magnet for every series I do, and I give all of them to my subscribers. Because a fiction collection is even better than a single short story. And since all my fiction takes place in the same universe, that makes it easy for me to bundle them all together.

And that's just for fiction. Non-fiction has their own list of other possibilities. In that realm, people usually like checklists, workbooks, daily/weekly plans, etc.

The length of a reader magnet can vary, but I would recommend at least one short story totaling more than 5K words. That's the bare minimum. If you can do more, do more. The more value you add for the reader, the more likely they are to subscribe to your list. That is why I have one new reader magnet for each new series.

2

HOW TO ACTUALLY CREATE YOUR READER MAGNET

Let's start by talking about how to actually produce one of these reader magnets. This is one of the most powerful tools in your author toolkit, especially when you're just starting out.

In this chapter, we'll walk through the entire process, from research to formatting, ensuring you end up with a reader magnet that will bring in a steady flow of subscribers.

Genre Research with Publisher Rocket

Before you dive into writing your reader magnet, it's crucial to understand your genre inside and out. This is where a tool like Publisher Rocket comes in handy. If you're not familiar with it, Publisher Rocket is a software that helps authors research keywords, categories, and competition on Amazon. It's an invaluable tool for understanding what readers in your genre are looking for.

Here's how to use Publisher Rocket for your reader magnet research:

1. Open Publisher Rocket and navigate to the Keyword Search feature.

2. Enter keywords related to your genre. For example, if you're writing urban fantasy, you might try "urban fantasy," "paranormal detective," or "magic in the city."

3. Look at the results. Pay attention to:

   - Search volume: How many people are searching for these terms?

   - Competitiveness: How hard would it be to rank for these keywords?

   - Average monthly earnings: This gives you an idea of how lucrative these niches are.

4. Next, use the Category Search feature to find relevant categories for your book.

5. Look at the top books in these categories. What are their titles like? What themes do they cover?

6. Use the Competition Analyzer to dig deeper into these top books. What are their prices? How many reviews do they have?

This research will give you valuable insights into what readers in your genre are looking for. Use this information to inform your reader magnet. If you see that "paranormal detective" books are popular in urban fantasy, consider making your reader magnet a short story about a detective solving a magical crime.

Additionally, I love to use AI tools to research a genre, as AI is phenomenal at picking up patterns like this. Simply ask the AI what the common conventions, tropes, and obligatory scenes are for a genre, and you'll have a long list of what to potentially include.

None of these, however, quite compare to actually reading in your genre, so don't forget to do that as well.

Remember, your reader magnet should be representative of your main work. If someone enjoys your reader magnet, they should enjoy your full book or series. So use this research to ensure your reader magnet aligns with what's popular in your genre.

Finding a Good Plot Formula

Now that you've done your research, it's time to start plotting your reader magnet. While it's not strictly necessary to follow a specific formula, I find it incredibly helpful, especially for shorter works like reader magnets. It keeps the story focused and prevents it from ballooning into something much larger than intended.

For short stories, I'm a big fan of the Lester Dent Plot Formula. Dent was a prolific pulp fiction author, best known for creating the character Doc Savage. His formula is designed to create a gripping, action-packed story in about 6,000 words - perfect for a reader magnet!

Here's a simplified version of the Lester Dent Plot Formula:

1. First 1,500 words:

   - Introduce your hero and put them in trouble.

   - Introduce the villain and their conflict with the hero.

   - End with a hook to keep readers engaged.

2. Second 1,500 words:

   - Hero tries to solve the problem but gets into worse trouble.

   - More conflict with the villain.

   - Another hook.

3. Third 1,500 words:

   - Hero makes progress but faces even bigger obstacles.

   - Hero seems to be defeated.

- Biggest hook yet.

4. Final 1,500 words:

- Hero uses their skills to defeat the villain.

- Wrap up the story, but maybe leave a thread for future stories.

This formula works particularly well for reader magnets that tie into your larger book or series. It allows you to create a brief, action-heavy story that gives readers a taste of your world and characters without giving away too much of your main plot.

For example, if your main book is about a wizard detective solving a major magical crime, your reader magnet could be about a smaller case they solved previously. This gives readers a feel for your writing style, introduces them to your main character, and leaves them wanting more - which is exactly what you want from a reader magnet!

Options to Write

When it comes to actually writing your reader magnet, you have several options. Let's break them down:

Writing It Yourself

This is the most straightforward option. You know your world and characters best, after all. If you choose to write it yourself, here's the process I recommend:

1. **Brainstorming:** Jot down all your ideas. Don't censor yourself at this stage - let your creativity flow!

2. **Characters:** Flesh out your characters. What are their goals? Their fears? Their quirks? Understand that you probably don't want more than one major character for a short story, and that character might not go through a full character arc. However, it can involve a single step in a character arc, or a particular question or decision that they're wrestling with.

3. **Worldbuilding:** Even for a short story, you need to know your world. What are the rules of magic? What's the political situation? What's the weather like? What's the floor plan for the building your scene takes place in?

4. **Synopsis:** Write a brief summary of your story. This should be no more than 2-3 paragraphs.

5. **Outline:** Expand your synopsis into a full outline. Use the Lester Dent formula or another structure to guide you.

6. **Beats:** Break your outline down into individual scenes or "beats." If you really want to go deep on

your outline, or if you're using AI, you can do this. However, you may also find that your high-level outline is enough, without having to go deeper.

7. **Writing:** Now you're ready to write! Use your outline/beats as a guide, but don't be afraid to deviate if the story takes you in a different direction.

8. **Editing:** Once you've finished your first draft, it's time to edit. Look for plot holes, inconsistencies, and areas where you can tighten up your prose.

Using AI

If you're comfortable with AI tools, they can be a huge help in creating your reader magnet. I actually teach people how to write with AI, following the same steps I outlined above. While AI can't do all the work for you, it can get you 50% of the way there, which can really help with decision fatigue. But it will still be your responsibility to take it up to the next notch with your editing and guidance.

Remember, if you're using AI, the goal is to enhance your creativity, not replace it. Use it as a productivity tool to spark ideas and overcome writer's block, but make sure the final product is uniquely yours.

Hiring a Ghostwriter

There's a third option to produce your reader magnet: hiring a ghostwriter. Sometimes I find this useful if I'm pressed for time and want to focus on the more important aspects (like the actual book). Here are some pros and cons of hiring a ghostwriter:

Pros:

- Saves you time

- Can be high quality if you hire a good writer

- Allows you to focus on your main work

Cons:

- Can be expensive

- May not capture your voice perfectly

- Requires clear communication to ensure the writer understands your vision

Formatting

Once you've written your reader magnet, it's time to format it. Remember, this is often a reader's first impression of your work, so it needs to look professional.

Personally, I use Atticus for formatting. It's a powerful tool that allows you to create beautiful ebooks and print books.

Here's a quick guide to formatting your reader magnet with Atticus:

1. Create a new project in Atticus.

2. Import your manuscript.

3. Choose a theme that fits your genre. Atticus has a wide selection of pre-made themes, or you can create your own.

4. Customize your front matter (title page, copyright page, etc.).

5. Add chapter breaks where necessary.

6. Preview your book to make sure everything looks good.

7. Export as an ebook (EPUB format).

Remember, your reader magnet should look just as professional as your published books. Pay attention to details like font choice, paragraph spacing, and chapter headings. A well-formatted ebook shows readers that you take your craft seriously.

Book Covers

We'll dive deeper into book covers later on, but it's worth mentioning here because it's crucial for your reader magnet.

A good cover can be the difference between someone signing up for your mailing list or scrolling past.

Your reader magnet cover should:

- Clearly convey your genre

- Be visually appealing

- Look professional

- Match the style of your main book's cover (if it's related)

Remember, this cover will often be displayed in a small size (like in email signatures or social media posts), so make sure it's clear and readable even when small.

If you're not a designer, consider hiring a professional. There are many affordable options out there, and the investment is worth it. My topic recommendation for a reader magnet is using a service like GetCovers.

I suppose if you're really strapped for cash, you could use AI to generate the reader magnet cover, but I would only do that until you've earned enough money to pay for a more professional cover. And you'll still want to get a designer to add the text and everything to make it look professional.

Creating a reader magnet might seem like a lot of work, especially when you're eager to get started on your main book. But trust me, it's worth the effort. A good reader magnet is the key to building your mailing list, and if you can get that ball rolling *before* you've even released your book, then when you do release your first book, you'll already have an audience for it.

Don't get too caught up in the details at this stage. The most important thing is to produce your reader magnet. It doesn't have to be perfect - you can always update it later. What matters is that it gives readers a taste of your writing and leaves them wanting more.

Step 2: The Newsletter

3

WHAT TO DO WITH THE READER MAGNET?

So let's assume you now have a reader magnet, what do you do with it? Do you simply post a link on your website and social media pages and hope that people randomly stumble across it?

Remember, you don't just want people on your newsletter, you want the *right* people on your newsletter. We'll talk about why that's important in a later chapter, but for now, just trust me that if you are targeting sweet romance, you want sweet romance readers on your newsletter, and no one else.

That means, you need to go where the readers are.

As of this writing, the best way I know how to get new subscribers with only a reader magnet and no book out, is to use a service like Bookfunnel or StoryOrigin.

These are services built to make it easier to deliver these reader magnets and other books. And they do a terrific job at that, easily walking the reader through whatever steps they have to take in order to load that book/short story onto their respective devices. For a small fee, you can also set up your book so that people have to subscribe to your newsletter to get it. I actually recommend this. Bookfunnel integrates easily with most email subscription services. StoryOrigin does this too.

However, these services also have another key service that I highly recommend for authors who are just starting out: their promotions.

Basically, what you do is you join other authors in group promotions of their work, usually based around a certain genre. All you have to do is find a promotion that is the genre you're looking for, enlist your own reader magnet, then send it out to your email and social media. All the other authors do the same, and if your reader magnet is set up correctly, everyone who signs up to get that particular book will be signed up to your email.

Now, of course, some of those people will unsubscribe from your list the moment they have your free thing. But in my experience, most do not. If you're offering them sufficient value, they won't want to leave your newsletter. And I've found that many of those who sign up through these promotions are the kind of readers that are looking for fresh, new things. Some in the industry would call them whale readers.

I personally use StoryOrigin because of its many features and affordability (as of this writing). But Bookfunnel is also a great option, and in some cases it might be worth using all three at one point because each one will have an audience of different readers. But that might be overkill.

But where else should you put your reader magnet?

Your reader magnet should be in more places than one. Once your first book is out, for example, a link to your reader magnet should be in the back, or front, or both. People who sign up via this link are far more likely to be engaged with your work than those who sign up through Bookfunnel promotions. After all, those who signed up via Bookfunnel (or any of the other services) could just be the type of people looking for free reads. People who sign up from the link in your book, however, have already paid money for your work! If they do that AND sign up for your newsletter, chances are they will pay money for your stuff again.

Some authors also use Facebook groups as an alternative to email newsletters, and provide a link to the reader magnet on that group. As of right now, Facebook groups are still good. They usually get good interaction, and allow your readers to interact with each other, which they can't do via email. But that is only the case for now. It is likely that over time, just like with Facebook pages, the groups will lose their usefulness. So if you go with a Facebook group, I would recommend doing that *in addition* to your email list.

Lastly, there is also the choice of paying money to get email subscribers. The best way to do this is through Facebook ads. Mark Dawson has a great video series on how to do this. However, though it's certainly possible to pay for these subscribers, I actually do not recommend you do so. These subscribes are usually very low in activity rate. Most will never buy your book even after they've subscribed. I don't know why this is, but that is the case for me. Some authors are able to get it to work (like Mark), but in most cases, your dollars are better spent on something like a good cover, or for advertising your book.

Which Email Service to Get?

Lastly, let's talk about which email service you should go with. The short answer is, whichever works best for you, but many starting authors have no idea what that means, so let me give you my recommendation.

It used to be that Mailchimp was the main email service provider that most people went with. They were free up to 2000 subscribers, and had all the features you needed. The logic was, once you got over 2000 subscribers, you would probably be making enough to cover the costs of paying for an email list.

Unfortunately, Mailchimp has undergone a number of changes and is now, in my opinion, not the best place for a new author to start.

For brand new authors, I recommend using MailerLite. They are free up to 1000 subscribers, and even once you're on the paid plan, they are much cheaper than the other options. They also offer all the special features you might need, some of which Mailchimp no longer provides to free users, like automation.

Now, there is a lot more I could say about newsletters, but if you want to learn more, there is one resource I recommend above the others, and that is Tammi Labrecque's book *Newsletter Ninja*. She goes in depth on all of the advice I've given so far, and into some things I haven't talked about much. You'll learn more about automation, writing engaging headlines, as well as what you should email and how often you should do so. Go check it out!

4

NEWSLETTER SWAPS

We've talked about newsletters, and why they're so important. I also talked about newsletter promotions through StoryOrigin or Bookfunnel, which are great ways to build an audience when you have none. And you've heard me talk about just how important a reader magnet is to attract your audiences.

But what I haven't talked about is newsletter swaps. Newsletter swaps are ways in which authors cross-promote each other, and cross pollinate their newsletters.

It works like this. Basically, if I have a new book I'm launching, I go to a bunch of other authors and ask if they would share my book in their newsletter. In exchange, I agree to put one of their books in my newsletter. Authors then respond with the book they would like promoted. We settle the details, such as the timing, and then make sure to promote when we say we'll promote.

Even if you don't have a new release, this can be a great way to get steady readership of your books. And here's the most important aspect of newsletter swaps: it is by far the best marketing option for your book that doesn't cost you any money. If an author is asking you to pay for their swap, DO NOT USE THEM. Swaps should be free, and if someone tells you otherwise, they might be trying to take advantage of you.

As of this writing, the best place to find newsletter swaps is in author Facebook groups set up for that express purpose, or through services like StoryOrigin. There are several of them out there. Just search Facebook for "Newsletter Swap" or "Author Cross Promotion" and something is likely to come up. And chances are good there will also be one or two groups specifically for the genre you write in.

Now, note that you can use newsletter swaps for both your reader magnet *and* your book. If you haven't written your book yet, and all you have is a reader magnet, then I strongly recommend you get into a rhythm of submitting your reader magnet for any promotions and newsletter swaps that you can qualify for. If you can set a steady schedule of emails you plan to send out, and how many newsletter swaps you want to participate in each newsletter, then doing so steadily will eventually pay off with hundreds, and perhaps even thousands of new subscribers before you've even launched a book.

Now you may be wondering what to do if you have no audience yet. How can you ask someone to share your book if you share theirs with an audience of practically zero? Well, first of all, that's why I emphasized StoryOrigin or Book-funnel promotions earlier in this book. Those are great for getting readers. Secondly, if your book has a cool cover and blurb, and looks like it would be a good match for another author's audience, I've generally found that most are still willing to share. They're more interested in providing great value to their newsletter, and if your book looks like great value, then that's all they need to know. That said, you should still try to build your audience as much as possible so you can provide a sufficient exchange of sales.

How many swaps is too much? Presumably, if you have too many books listed in your newsletter, your readers will feel spammed or simply lose interest. Generally, I've found that 2-4 is about as many as you'll want to do in one email. I try to keep it around 2 shares per email, on average. And I try to send out about one email per week. However, I will often bump that number up to 4 per email if I'm preparing for a big launch.

That's one strategy you can use. The more swaps you have surrounding your book launch, the more Amazon will see that steady influx of sales as evidence that your book is good, and that they should promote it. So the more swaps you can get at launch, the better. I recommend starting months in advance, sharing other people's books with your newsletter in exchange for an IOU. Then, when you're finally ready to launch, you can coordinate with all those authors you shared, and get an avalanche of swaps all within a month's time.

The other common strategy is simply to use newsletter swaps as a way of keeping your book current. A couple swaps a month could keep your book from sliding too far down the rankings.

That said, these two strategies are best served after you've established yourself as an author. When you're just starting out, I would just focus on getting as many swaps as you can right around your launch, as well as 1-2 swaps per month (at least) to your reader magnet to build up that newsletter.

But like I said, if your book cover and blurb are really good, most authors will still agree to send your book out to their newsletter, even if you can't offer them as much value in return. So I say again, and I can't emphasize this enough, make sure your book cover and blurb are amazing and targeting the right audience.

5

WHAT TO PUT IN YOUR NEWSLETTERS

When it comes to email newsletters, many authors find themselves intimidated by the prospect of regularly communicating with their readers. The blank canvas of an email can seem daunting, especially when you're just starting out. But fear not! Crafting engaging emails for your subscribers is not as difficult as it might appear at first glance.

The key to successful email marketing lies in understanding that your newsletter is more than just a promotional tool—it's a way to build a relationship with your readers. This chapter will guide you through the various types of content you can include in your emails, helping you create a newsletter that your subscribers will eagerly anticipate.

Nurturing Your New Subscribers

If you've just started growing your email list through your reader magnet, it's crucial to engage with these new subscribers right away. These early interactions will set the tone for your relationship with your readers, so make them count.

Remember, these individuals have shown interest in your work by signing up for your newsletter. They're curious about you and your writing. Your job now is to nurture that curiosity and keep them engaged until your next book release—and beyond.

Regular communication is key. You want to stay fresh in your readers' minds without overwhelming them. The following are just *some* of the suggestions that I would make for the content of your emails. It's certainly not limited to these, but this is what I'd start with:

New Release Announcements

One of the most exciting emails you'll send (both for you and your readers) is the announcement of a new book release. This is your moment to shine, to share the culmination of your hard work with your most dedicated fans.

When crafting a new release announcement, consider including the following elements:

1. **Eye-catching subject line:** Make it clear that this is a new release announcement. Something like "It's here! [Book Title] is now available!" can work well.

2. **Cover image:** Prominently display your book cover. Visual elements can greatly increase engagement.

3. **Book blurb:** Include a short, enticing description of your book. This should be polished and compelling—think of it as your elevator pitch.

4. **Purchase links:** Make it easy for readers to buy your book by including direct links to major retailers.

5. **Launch special:** Consider offering a special deal for your subscribers, like a limited-time discount or a bonus short story.

6. **Personal note:** Share your excitement about the release.

Remember, this is not just an announcement—it's a celebration. Invite your readers to share in your joy. You might even encourage them to spread the word by sharing the news on social media.

Pre-Release Announcements

Building anticipation for your upcoming release can be just as important as the release announcement itself. Pre-release announcements give your readers something to look forward to and can help generate early buzz for your book.

Here are some ideas for pre-release announcement emails:

1. **Cover reveal:** Make an event out of revealing your book cover. You could even tease it with snippets or silhouettes in earlier emails.

2. **Pre-order availability:** Let readers know when and where they can pre-order your book (if you plan to).

3. **Sneak peeks:** Share a short excerpt from your upcoming book. Choose a passage that will leave readers wanting more.

4. **Behind-the-scenes:** Give readers insight into your writing process for this book. What inspired you? What challenges did you face?

5. **Countdown emails:** As the release date approaches, send emails marking the countdown. "Only one week until [Book Title] is in your hands!"

Pre-release announcements are all about building excitement. Use this opportunity to make your readers feel like insiders, privy to exclusive information about your upcoming work.

Personal Updates

While your books are undoubtedly the main focus of your writing career, your readers are also interested in you as a person. Sharing personal updates can help foster a deeper connection with your audience. In fact, besides your book announcements, these might be the most important emails you send, because it builds that connection between you and the reader.

Here are some ideas for personal update emails:

1. **Writing progress:** Share your word count goals and achievements. Let readers know how your current project is coming along.

2. **Behind-the-scenes:** Give readers a glimpse into your writing process. Share photos of your writing space or your planning methods.

3. **Reading recommendations:** Talk about books you're currently reading or have recently enjoyed. Your readers likely share your taste in literature.

4. **Life events:** Share significant events in your life, like moving to a new city or adopting a pet (pets, for some reason, are huge for newsletters). J

5. **Challenges and victories:** Be honest about the struggles you face as a writer, and celebrate your successes, no matter how small.

6. **Q&A sessions:** Invite readers to ask you questions, then answer them in your email.

Personal updates help your readers see you as a real person, not just a name on a book cover. This can foster loyalty and encourage readers to support your work long-term.

Story Bible Info

For authors writing in genres like fantasy or science fiction, sharing elements from your story bible can be a great way to keep readers engaged between book releases. This is especially effective if you're writing a series or multiple books set in the same world. And some of these work for authors of other genres as well.

Consider sharing:

1. **Character profiles:** Dive deep into your characters' backstories, motivations, and quirks.

2. **World maps:** If your story takes place in a fictional world, share maps to help readers visualize the setting.

3. **Historical timelines:** Provide context for your story by sharing key historical events from your world.

4. **Magic systems:** Explain how magic works in your world, including its rules and limitations.

5. **Creature bestiaries:** Describe the unique creatures that inhabit your world.

6. **Cultural details:** Share information about the different cultures, religions, or societies in your story world.

Sharing story bible information gives your readers a deeper understanding of your fictional world. It can enhance their reading experience and keep them invested in your story between book releases.

AI Concept Art

With the rise of AI art generation tools, authors now have a new way to visually represent elements of their stories. Sharing AI-generated concept art can be an engaging addition to your newsletters.

Side note: Non-AI Art is also fine here, if you've hired someone to do your art. However, I'm working under the assumption that you can't afford the thousands of dollars to do this (nor would it be a smart idea to spend that much if you're just starting out), so in that case I recommend going with AI for now, until you can afford those artists.

Here are some ideas for incorporating AI concept art:

1. **Character portraits:** Use AI to generate images of your main characters. Discuss how closely they match your mental image.

2. **Scene illustrations:** Create visual representations of key scenes from your books.

3. **Setting depictions:** Generate images of important locations in your story world.

4. **Creature designs:** If your story features unique creatures, use AI to bring them to life visually.

5. **Object showcases:** Generate images of important objects or artifacts from your story.

When sharing AI art, always be transparent about its origin. Explain how you used AI to create the images and what prompts you used. This can even be an interesting behind-the-scenes look at your creative process.

Repurposed Blog/Video Content

If you maintain a blog or YouTube channel in addition to your newsletter, you can repurpose this content for your emails. This not only provides value to your email subscribers but also drives traffic to your other platforms.

My favorite way to do this is actually through using AI.

I'll take the transcript of a video, or an entire blog post, and post it into a chatbot like ChatGPT or Claude with the following prompt: *Take the following video transcript/blog/social media post and convert it into an email newsletter: [INSERT CONTENT HERE]*

And even a simple prompt like that is enough to get me a full newsletter to use for the day.

Just make sure you're still thoroughly reading it through and making sure it sounds natural and accurate.

Balancing Marketing and Value

While it's important to promote your books, it's equally crucial not to overwhelm your readers with constant marketing messages. A good rule of thumb is to follow the 80/20 rule: 80% of your emails should provide value (personal updates, story information, etc.), while only 20% should be direct marketing (new releases, sales, etc.).

This approach ensures that your readers don't feel like they're being constantly sold to. Instead, they'll see your newsletter as a valuable resource, making them more receptive when you *do* have something to promote.

The key is to make your readers look forward to your emails, not dread them as just another marketing message in their inbox.

Setting a Schedule

Consistency is key when it comes to email newsletters. Your readers should know when to expect to hear from you. This not only helps you stay on track but also trains your audience to anticipate and open your emails.

Here are some tips for setting and maintaining an email schedule:

1. **Choose a frequency:** Decide how often you want to send emails. I recommend no less than once a month, but once a week is ideal for maintaining regular contact with your readers.

2. **Pick a day and time:** Choose a specific day of the

week and time to send your emails. Consistency helps your readers know when to expect your messages.

3. **Use an editorial calendar:** Plan your email content in advance. This helps ensure you always have something to say when it's time to send an email.

4. **Be flexible:** While consistency is important, don't be afraid to send additional emails for important announcements or time-sensitive information.

5. **Communicate changes:** If you need to change your email frequency, let your subscribers know in advance.

6. **Quality over quantity:** It's better to send fewer, high-quality emails than to spam your list with low-value content just to stick to a schedule.

Remember, the goal is to find a rhythm that works for both you and your readers. You want to stay fresh in their minds without overwhelming them. And don't be afraid to experiment, because you may find that something that works for one audience won't work for another, and that you may have to tweak some of my advice here.

Step 3: The Book

MythHQ

Myth HQ, LLC

6

WRITE A SERIES

T his is some advice that I present cautiously, and you will see me almost contradict it later on. Writing a series is one of the more crucial things you can do if you want to get a return on investment.

Return on investment (ROI) is a fancy term to mean getting your money back. When you release a book, you will likely spend money on a cover, some editing, and maybe some advertising. Writing a series is particularly important for that last expense.

Based on the current state of advertising, you will likely lose money if and when you decide to run ads on your bo ok...IF it's just one book. Let's say you spend $5 advertising, and only make one sale. Let's say your book was priced at $ 2.99, which means (based on Amazon's current royalty rate), you'd get about $2 of that. But wait? Spending $5 to get $2? How can that be successful??

Well, let's assume that book has three more books that follow. If the reader goes on to buy the set, that's $8 total that you get to pocket. Now, of course, not everyone is going to buy the other books, and there are whole courses devoted to calculating the profitability of your ads. I'm not going to get into that here. The point is, if you have books in a series, you will make more money than if you only had one.

As a side note, I believe the same is also true of having multiple series. If all you have is one series, there are going to be fewer readers that give you a chance. But if you have three or four series, then they've just found a new potential treasure trove of escapism at their finger tips. Readers like this.

Now the reason I started this chapter by saying I approach this subject cautiously is because of a mistake I made in my first complete series. In my case, I wrote too *many* books in a series. My first series was comprised of no less than 8 books (and one prequel short story). Now, this would have been great had the series been the next *Twilight*. But unfortunately (or perhaps fortunately depending on how you look at it), my books were not the next *Twilight*. Oh yes, I sold a thousand copies in my first month, which isn't bad, to say the least. But as that number dropped from month to month, I was left with several books to finish, and not enough money to really motivate me to finish them.

This goes back to my two warnings in a previous chapter, that you will (A) likely not make a lot of money from your first series, and (B) your first book(s) will not be all that great.

By the time I finished that series, I cringed when reading the first book.

That is why I strongly recommend that your first series be no more than three books. Maybe four. You will learn a lot, and I mean A LOT, while writing those books. And you'll have a complete series in far less time. That means you will be able to take all you learned in writing those three books and apply all that to your next series, which is likely to do much better.

Now, there's actually another strategy that I'm going to recommend to you today, one that I didn't do personally, but I've seen it work for a lot of authors, and it's a great way to jumpstart a career when you're just starting out.

So let's dive into that next...

7

"Splitting" Your Book Into Four Novellas

This is one of the greatest strategies that I've ever heard for a beginning author and is 100% the path I would take if I were starting over today.

You see, we've established the importance of a series to make money long-term.

But I've also established that I wouldn't start with more than a trilogy or so of books, because by the time you finish those books, you'll have improved a lot as an author and won't want to be stuck in the same series for much longer.

So here's the solution: Write one book, and split it into 3-4 novellas.

Yes, I'm talking about literally going from one title to four.

Here are some of the reasons why I recommend this:

It Works for Traditional and Self-publishing

One of my idols, Brandon Sanderson, wrote 13 books before he was published. All 13 of those were separate books, the first in their series.

And this makes sense, because he was trying to get traditionally published, and it's not exactly recommended to start writing a sequel to a book if you don't even have a publisher for the first book yet.

So he got really good at writing the first book in a series.

Well, let's say you'd like to try for traditional publishing as well. You could write your book, shop it around, and if after 1-2 years of doing that (traditionally publishing can take a while to get back to you), you could split it into 4 novellas and self-publish them instead. Then, even though you only wrote 1 book, you still have 4 titles that give you at least some of the benefits of a series, without having to write a few more books.

It Gives You Experience with Book 1s

Book 1 is almost always the most important book in a series, because it's the book that has to hook the reader. If the reader doesn't like it, they won't move on to read the rest of the series.

By only writing book 1s, then splitting them into 4 novellas, you get more practice working on those book 1s, while also getting the benefits of a series.

It Increases the Titles You Have

Now a savvy reader will see past this, but it's important to note that many readers will not start reading books from a new author unless they can see that the author in question is well established. And they can tell if you're established by the number of books you have (as well as other factors like the reviews, the quality of the covers, etc.).

Well, by splitting a book into sections, you can create the illusion of having multiple titles, which is super helpful when you're just starting out. Of course, the goal is to eventually write a lot more books, but when you only have 3, for example, it's nice to write 3 books and have 12 titles on your Amazon store.

It Lets Your Calculate Read-through

Now THIS is the most important reason why I would do this if I were to start over today.

Splitting your book into 4 novellas allows you to calculate the read through for that book.

So basically, you look at the number of people who read the first novella, then the number of people who read the second, then the third, and so on.

If a high percentage of people reading the first novella are moving on to read the second novella as well, then that's a good sign that people actually liked your first novella.

And the best part is, you can compare the read through of one book compared to another. So let's say you write three books, then split them into 4 novellas each, for a total of 12 novellas. Then you calculate the read-through for all three "series". and find that one of your books is performing a lot better than the others.

That's a good sign that your readers love that book more, and if you're to continue on to write more books in the same series, I'd do it for that book, because more people are reading past the first novella.

How to Calculate Read-through

To calculate the read-through rate from novella 1 to novella 2, you would use the following formula:

Read-through rate = (Number of buyers for novella 2) / (Number of buyers for novella 1) * 100%

This calculation gives you the percentage of readers who continued from the first novella to the second novella in a series. Here's a step-by-step breakdown:

1. Determine the number of readers who read novella 1 (usually the number of purchases, but you'll want to factor in the page reads from Kindle Unlimited if you're enrolled in KU)

2. Determine the number of readers who read novella 2

3. Divide the number of novella 2 readers by the number of novella 1 readers

4. Multiply the result by 100 to get a percentage

For example, if 100 people read novella 1 and 75 people read novella 2, the calculation would be:

Read-through rate = (75 / 100) * 100% = 75%

This means 75% of readers continued from novella 1 to novella 2.

Once again, this metric is useful for authors and publishers to gauge reader engagement and the success of a novella series. A higher read-through rate generally indicates that readers enjoyed the first novella enough to continue with the series.

So to wrap it all up, I would strongly recommend that you split your book into four parts, with each becoming its own novella.

However, there are dangers to this. For example, you want to make sure that each part ends in a place that at least feels like an ending, and not that it's just a piece cut from a larger book (even though it is). So you might have to shift some things about the beginnings and ends of each novella to feel more like a complete story.

To help with this, I developed an outline template called the Plot Module that I believe is perfect for this. More on that in the next chapter.

8

THE PLOT MODULE

I have a whole book on the Plot Module that goes into far more depth on each chapter, but I thought it would be an appropriate thing to include a brief summary of it here, so you can see how I would divide your first book into 4 novellas.

Now, obviously, your book might use a completely different structure, or you might not use structure at all. But I've found that a lot of newer authors really benefit from a rigid structure that gives you everything you need to know to write a solid book.

I benefitted from such a structure when I was starting out, and the Plot Module is the pinnacle of what I wish I had even then.

The Plot Module is designed to have everything you need for a complete plot with a central protagonist. It tells you every single thing that needs to happen in each chapter. While the model is flexible, and you can choose to rearrange or delete some scenes as needed, I stronger recommend that beginner authors try following these steps closely for those first few books.

If you are splitting your book into 4 novellas, I would end them exactly at the end of each act, with 10 chapters per novella (not counting the prologue and/or after-credit scene). Each of these usually ends with a big moment for the main character, and therefore can be used to highlight how far they've come so far, and the growth that they've experienced, which is a great way to end a novella.

So without further ado, here is a basic summary of the Plot Module:

Act 1:

- **Prologue (optional):** The prologue opens with a vivid image representing the central conflict or antagonist, showing the troubled state of the world. It sets the tone for the genre and conflict level of the story. While it may not directly involve the protagonist, it is thematically linked to them.

- **Chapter 1 – The Unusual Day:** The protagonist and their ordinary world are introduced through an opening image that reveals their flaw and setting. The protagonist wants something they believe will improve their life but faces an obstacle preventing them from obtaining it. The protagonist's need, flaw, friends, and family are introduced, and they have a "save the cat" moment to become likable to the reader.

- **Chapter 2 – Mystery and Theme:** An unusual event foreshadows future problems and may present a mystery, but the protagonist is distracted and fails to grasp its ramifications. More friends and family members are introduced, and the protagonist's unresolved emotional issues and flaws are further explored. The theme is stated by someone other than the protagonist, hinting at what they need to overcome, but the protagonist ignores this life lesson.

- **Chapter 3 – Link to the Antagonist:** In the protagonist's home, work, or play environment, they face a challenge, threat, or opportunity related to the antagonist, linking the two. The mystery deepens, and the event may be presented as an opportunity to the protagonist.

- **Chapter 4 – Grasping at Straws:** The protagonist's desire intensifies, and their flaw becomes more evident as they criticize their ordinary world. They are not yet honest with themselves about their true needs.

- **Chapter 5 – The Hint of Death:** In another of the protagonist's environments, it becomes clear that if they continue living as they are, they will eventually

die (literally, socially, financially, or in their relationships) and never find true happiness. This scene
summarizes the insights from previous scenes.

- **Chapter 6 – Inciting Incident:** A dramatic event
  disrupts the status quo in the ordinary world, creating conflict that cannot resolve itself. The incident
  deeply impacts the protagonist but not enough to
  make them leave their ordinary world.

- **Chapter 7 – The Call to Adventure:** The protagonist is forced to focus on the new issues and fallout from the inciting incident, which interferes with
  their previous goals. The protagonist's reaction and
  emotional state in response to the call are explored,
  showing how they push back against it.

- **Chapter 8 – Meeting the Mentor:** A mentor (a person, crucial information, or supernatural aid) enters
  the protagonist's life, encouraging them to take action and heed the call to adventure. The mentor provides tools, training, information, or support needed for the journey and hints at the protagonist's
  fatal flaw, which the protagonist ignores or fails to
  recognize.

- **Chapter 9 – Refusal of the Call:** The protagonist
  refuses to accept the call to adventure despite the
  growing intrigue, tension, and supernatural events.

They attempt to ignore the challenge of the new world, building regret and doubt while finding it increasingly difficult to continue in the ordinary world.

- **Chapter 10 – Pull Out the Rug:** The protagonist tries to fix issues in the ordinary world to resist the call to adventure, but an event pulls the rug out from under them, forcing them into action. This event is more personal, such as a kidnapping, death of a loved one, loss of financial security, or being driven from home. The protagonist must take on the mission or face a life-threatening situation, and the stakes and tensions are high, hooking the reader.

Act 2A

- **Chapter 11 – First Plot Point:** The protagonist actively chooses to enter the new and uncomfortable world, which may involve an environmental change or simply trying something new. This is a significant turning point in the story, and there is no going back to the ordinary world. The protagonist still has their flaw and desires, which hinder their progress, but they are willing to push through into the new world.

- **Chapter 12 – Enemies & Allies:** The protagonist's

new life in the uncomfortable world is introduced, making them feel like a fish out of water. Any remaining characters, including the main antagonist, are introduced, and character archetypes such as the side character, ally, or love interest are established. The protagonist's new role is defined, and they may face antagonism and friction with side characters.

- **Chapter 13 – The B Story:** The protagonist spends time with the B story character, who helps them recognize their flaw. It is made clear that there is no going back, and the protagonist is given reasons and motivation to continue. The theme is restated, often as advice on how to succeed, though the protagonist may overlook or not fully understand it.

- **Chapter 14 – Games & Trials:** The exciting aspects of the new world are presented, allowing the protagonist to explore and learn to navigate it. Lingering friction with side characters persists, and the protagonist undergoes training or learning to harness their abilities in their new role. The protagonist faces a trial and either succeeds or fails, providing another glimpse of their flaw. This chapter offers an opportunity to wow readers through wonder and deliver on the story's premise.

- **Chapter 15 – No More Games:** The protagonist attempts a second trial and seemingly fails, but still experiences growth and learns valuable lessons. The cost of failure is more pronounced, and the protagonist experiences frustration and self-doubt.

- **Chapter 16 – Earning Respect:** The protagonist succeeds in the third trial, proving they are not completely useless and experiencing a small victory. This boosts their self-confidence and may gain the attention of allies and enemies. The protagonist's overconfidence may lead to the first pinch point, and the B character reminds them of the life lesson they need to learn, which the protagonist clearly has not yet learned.

- **Chapter 17 – First Pinch Point:** The protagonist and antagonist (or forces of evil) have their first major interaction, which can be a literal or nonliteral battle. The antagonist's motives are tied to the protagonist, who still has little understanding of the situation but finds themselves at the center of the conflict. The protagonist survives but may not win, and the stakes become clearer and more dire. This is a significant turning point in the story, and the protagonist is humbled by the event and their realization of the actual situation. A plot twist may be introduced.

- **Chapter 18 – Problem Revealed:** The protagonist feels overwhelmed as they realize how much they don't know, as revealed by the previous chapter's challenges. Allies may have withheld information about the true level of threat, or the protagonist may learn from a trusted advisor or other individual. The protagonist confronts the allies, demanding answers, but may initially be brushed off or told they are not ready.

- **Chapter 19 – Truth & Ultimatum:** The protagonist learns critical new information that changes their worldview, revealing the full extent of the antagonist's forces, the backstory of the problem, and what they are up against. They may gain a new perspective on the allies or even sympathy for the antagonist. With this complete information, the protagonist must decide whether to continue "all in" or find a way back to the ordinary world. A plot twist or revelation may cause them to second-guess their decisions.

- **Chapter 20 – Midpoint:** This single scene marks either a false victory or a false defeat and is the point when the protagonist decides to be more proactive and take action. They form a new goal and are forced to confront who they are and what they need to change to succeed. The protagonist fully engages with their flaw and realizes they need to change, even if they can't yet. The stakes of the story are raised, and the A and B stories intersect in this major turning point.

Act 2B

- **Chapter 21 – External Demons Close In:** The protagonist faces external demons, such as the antagonist or their forces, who regroup after the first pinch point and midpoint. Evidence or speculation of the bad guys' preparations is shown, even if they are not seen directly. This chapter may also introduce more complications for the protagonist and presents an opportunity for a plot twist.

- **Chapter 22 – Things Get Worse:** Just when it seems things can't get worse, they do, possibly through a betrayal, plot twist, or shocking revelation. The stakes are heightened, and the protagonist barely survives, only because they have started to doubt the benefits of their flaw.

- **Chapter 23 – Internal Demons Close In:** The protagonist's internal doubt and the consequences of their flaw become apparent, causing them to mess up relationships, self-sabotage, or fight to return to the ordinary world. The external demons may continue to close in, exploiting or magnifying the protagonist's internal demons.

- **Chapter 24 – Plan of Attack:** The protagonist and their allies regroup, and the protagonist decides to go all-in and formulate a plan to confront the problem revealed earlier. They work with allies to use their new information and understand the antagonist's plans and what needs to be done to stop them.

- **Chapter 25 – Crucial Role:** The protagonist is given a crucial role, providing them an opportunity to prove themselves and be tested in the real world. Other characters begin to trust the protagonist, who must be responsible for what happens to build emotion.

- **Chapter 26 – Second Pinch Point:** A second battle with the antagonist or their forces occurs, often instigated by the antagonist and taking the protagonist by surprise. This results from the protagonist's actions in the previous chapters. The protagonist is determined to see the battle through and feels responsible for the outcome, despite the slim chances of success. During the conflict, the protagonist realizes they have underestimated the antagonist's power.

- **Chapter 27 – All Is Lost:** The antagonist defeats the protagonist's forces, and their plans go horribly wrong. Being in direct contact with the antagonist's forces reveals the protagonist and allies' identities, leading to real consequences such as the death of an ally, permanent disfigurement, or loss of an important object, raising the stakes. The allies are at a loss of what to do next, and the failure is usually due to the protagonist's flaw or lack of knowledge.

- **Chapter 28 – Shocking Revelation:** The protagonist learns new information in their new predicament, and the antagonist's full plan or true identity is revealed. The protagonist may experience guilt and anger at themselves for failing or at the antagonist for outsmarting them. The stakes are raised as the worst has happened.

- **Chapter 29 – Giving Up:** Having lost the battle, the protagonist loses confidence and gives up, facing their Dark Night of the Soul. They underestimated the antagonist, their plan failed, and they lost their one shot at getting it right. They feel powerless, hopeless, and like a failure, with real fallout from their failure. The stakes are raised, and victory seems impossible.

- **Chapter 30 – Pep Talk:** The protagonist no longer

believes in themselves and needs someone to pull them out of their depressive cycle. They receive a pep talk, possibly encouragement from an ally or someone sharing a vulnerable story. The ally helps the protagonist realize their fatal flaw and how it has been a blind spot, though this may not be perfectly obvious yet. The pep talk rebuilds their confidence, reaffirms what is at stake, and presents the choice of how to move forward.

Act 3

- **Chapter 31 – Seizing the Sword:** The protagonist finds the courage to continue despite the impossible odds. A critical piece of information may be revealed, giving the protagonist and allies an extra boost. The protagonist gears up for the final battle, assembling needed assets and creating another plan of attack.

- **Chapter 32 – Gathering the Team:** The protagonist gathers their team through inspiration, possibly making amends with previously scorned allies. Despite some antagonism, the protagonist's increased confidence convinces the allies to help. Together, they coordinate their next steps and gather necessary tools.

- **Chapter 33 – Final Battle, First Stage:** The plan moves into motion with the first stage, the "Storming the Castle" moment. This part goes relatively smoothly, giving hope for the protagonist's success. Skills and information learned in Act 2A help the protagonist succeed, and subplots between the protagonist and ally characters may pay off.

- **Chapter 34 – Final Battle, Second Stage:** The protagonist and allies move on to the plan's next stage, which is more difficult but still goes relatively well. Once again, Act 2A skills and information aid the protagonist's success, and subplots may be resolved. The protagonist seems to have learned to reverse the flaw that held them back in Act 2A. Often, allies drop off by this scene, forcing the protagonist to continue alone.

- **Chapter 35 – Final Battle, Third Stage:** The protagonist enters the third stage of the final battle alone, thinking they understand their fatal flaw but not fully. Their overconfidence leads to their undoing, but they fight to save others or the world, raising the stakes. This is another "All is Lost" moment, with a final, unexpected plot twist giving the antagonist the upper hand.

- **Chapter 36 – Ultimate Defeat:** The protagonist

faces a humiliation scene at the antagonist's mercy. The antagonist reveals their full plan, tying up loose ends. The protagonist fully understands their flaw and lets go of what was holding them back, possibly with the antagonist pointing out the flaw. The protagonist has no hope of winning unless they face their fatal flaw.

- **Chapter 37 – The Drop:** The antagonist believes they have won, but the protagonist gains a new understanding of themselves and their fatal flaw, deciding to let it go or move past it. The protagonist's want versus need comes to a head, and they realize they may never achieve their want but will sacrifice it and fight anyway. The protagonist understands they must rid themselves of their flaw and embrace their new self to win.

- **Chapter 38 – Unexpected Victory:** The protagonist, having abandoned their flaw, executes a new plan that allows them to achieve success. They may have a secret weapon, item, ability, or hidden ally that was overlooked throughout the story. This secret thing, combined with their newly changed self, helps them escape trouble and achieve victory over the antagonist. More allies and characters may be sacrificed, possibly even the protagonist.

- **Chapter 39 – Bittersweet Reflection:** The protagonist has won the battle, leading to joyful celebration or bittersweet reflection. If part of a series, they may have driven off the antagonist or battled a powerful but lesser henchman. The protagonist is now a changed person.

- **Chapter 40 – Death of Self:** All remaining loose ends are tied up, including storylines and character arcs of other main characters and allies. This chapter should represent the protagonist's rebirth, showing how they sacrificed their own desires to save others and defeat the antagonist. This significant shift may deserve an acknowledgment ceremony or public recognition. If part of a series, hints of future challenges are included. The story ends with a closing image of the protagonist, complementing the opening image but showing their transformation.

- **After-Credit Scene (optional):** A closing image visually represents the upcoming conflict for future books or series, increasing the stakes, similar to a Marvel after-credit scene teasing upcoming films.

9

Write. That. Book.

Even with tools as powerful as the Plot Module, by far the most important thing you can do as an author, the thing that will give you the most results, is your writing. I cannot overstate this enough. You. Must. Write.

I'm as guilty as anyone of getting stuck in analysis paralysis, or excusing myself from writing for a day because I still need to "learn more", and I've also experienced burnout which put me out of commission for months. First of all, analysis is great, but there is a time and a place for it. If you have nothing written, then it has no place. You can create plans for your launch, try to learn advertising, see what other successful authors are doing to your heart's content. But if you don't actually have a book to market, none of that will do you any good. In terms of the 80/20 rule, writing books is the most important task you can do, and you should not delay.

Writing Even When It's Hard

Let's face it, writing is not an easy task. It's straight up challenging. If we aren't second guessing every word we write, we're dealing with constant distractions around the house, or we're worked to the bone at our day job and need a break.

There are many well-meaning authors out there who might suggest that if you have too much trouble writing, then maybe you don't really want it enough. Maybe you should find something else that brings you more joy. Now, while this is certainly going to be true for some people, most of those people would not have even considered becoming writers in the first place. The fact that you're reading this book tells me that's not the case. You want to be a writer, so if you're having trouble writing, it's likely from one or several issues.

Now let me preface this next bit by saying that I am not a psychologist, nor do I deal with any mental health issues (except a few mild yet unmedicated ADHD symptoms). But I know from interacting with others that these can be some of the hardest obstacles to overcome. As I do not have depression or clinical anxiety, or any number of mental illnesses, I feel a little uncomfortable even talking about the subject. And so I won't attempt to give much advice to those of you who struggle with these things. There are books out there that will do a better job than I can, and even better, consider seeing a therapist. They will help you.

That being said, there are two pieces of advice that I know can help anyone, regardless of the state of your mind.

Whether you're a person with a completely healthy brain who's simply suffering from writer's block, or someone battling severe depression, or someone who can't focus for more than a millisecond because of ADHD, one thing that can help you in all circumstances is: habits.

Form Writing Habits

There's a great book out there called *The Power of Habit* by Charles Duhigg. It's less of a self-help book and more of a psychology science volume, but it explains habits in detail, and gives very interesting case studies of why habits are the key to all we want to accomplish.

Studies have uncovered that willpower is a limited resource that we all possess, fueled by glucose and aided by certain things we do, like sleeping. Every time we make a decision, or resist that extra donut, or try to urge ourselves to write, we deplete a little bit of that willpower. Which literally means the harder we try, the less likely we'll be able to motivate ourselves later on. Thankfully, this limited resource does replenish itself with good rest and proper eating, and it can expand over time as you exercise it. But it's not a very reliable way to get stuff done, because the more we do in a day, the less we will be able to do later on.

That's where habits come in. Habits are certain practices that we've adopted so regularly that it no longer takes willpower to do them. That's why bad habits are so hard to break, because we often don't realize the process we go through to do that bad habit, and it takes a massive amounts of willpower and a slew of new replacement habits to break them. But good habits, well those can be invaluable to you.

The Power of Habit gives a number of interesting stories, but one of my favorites is about a man who, through a brain injury, lost all of his short term memory. That essentially left him non-functional. He couldn't remember anything that happened even a few short seconds ago. He was literally living in the moment. Over time, his wife would take him on walks around the block. They kept that up for some time. One day he simply left and went on the walk himself. His wife was frantic, since with his short term memory loss there was no possible way he would be able to find his way back. But he did. Why? Habits. His habits of going on the same walk every day were somehow able to override the fact that he could not remember the path. But he was still able to follow it because of habits.

That's how powerful habits can be. They can help you out even when depressed, distracted, sick, or otherwise less able to function. They allow you to write not only on your good days, but on your worst days as well.

Now, don't get me wrong, it's not easy. Forming a habit takes willpower, and as I mentioned above, willpower is in limited supply. That's why professionals will often encourage you to make small changes, a little bit at a time. Smaller habits will take less willpower to change, and you can slowly work up from there. This is the premise of the book *Atomic Habits* by James Clear, which is a book I highly recommend.

But getting back to writing. Author W. Somerset Maugham is quoted as saying "I write only when inspiration strikes. Fortunately it strikes every morning at nine o'clock sharp." I love this quote. I could frame it on my wall. In fact...hang on a second...

(undisclosed amount of time passes)

Anyway, what was I saying? Oh yes, writing habits. Inspiration is one of those things that we definitely need to write. When we don't have it, we call it writer's block. But in my experience, we often mistake writer's block for something it's not. The most common of these is that we just don't feel like writing, and we haven't developed a proper writing habit to combat this.

If you want to become a successful indie author, you must form a regular writing habit.

Some authors say you must stick to this every day. I'm less demanding and say you should do it at least every week day. Those are the days when your schedule is most likely to be regular. That will make it easier to stay regular. Weekends, in my experience, often have completely different schedules, and that can throw you off a bit. Personally, I take Sunday off, but I do write on Saturdays most of the time.

I recommend the books I've already mentioned for more on how to form lasting habits. It's a more involved process than you might think, but one of the most important to get right (lol, I first typed that as 'write'). Another one I would also recommend is *The Miracle Morning* by Hal Elrod. It's not about forming habits per se, but it is all about getting the most important things done in the morning, and that can include writing. That book was an eye opener for me, finally helping me realize that I could not only get out of bed and get a lot of awesome stuff done, but that I would look forward to waking up like a kid on Christmas.

I have personally incorporated a writing habit in my life, and it has made everything easier. The more I do it, the less willpower it takes for me to actually start putting my fingers to the keyboard. It's still hard sometimes, it likely always will be. But it is far easier to do today than it was a year ago, and I expect the same will be true a year from now.

Regular writing is absolutely essential if you want to finish your book, and finish many more books. As you will likely come to learn, writing a lot of books is one of the key strategies of a lot of successful indie authors. None of them have made it to the point where they're cranking out a million words a year without regular writing habits.

Be Healthier

This might not be advice you would have expected to see in a chapter about writing a book. But let me give you a personal story.

In April of 2018, I began to get a very uncomfortable growth in a very uncomfortable place. It was like a boil or a giant zit, but on an unprecedented scale, and this one did not back down. I let it get to the point where the pain of abscess was so great, it was the worst topical pain I had ever felt in my life.

I was eventually forced to go to the emergency room (my first time going there in my life) and they put me into surgery to drain the abscess. I was admitted to the hospital that night and later informed that I would likely be there to recover for a few days, not only so the doctor could check how the surgery was healing up but also because...surprise! I had type 2 diabetes and they needed to get my blood sugar under control.

Over the years I haven't been the healthiest person. I think my official BMI at that time would classify me as morbidly obese. I've known a lot about health as I've tried all the different things to improve, but on the whole my body has not been what it should be. Thankfully, I didn't have many serious health problems...until now.

With the type 2 diabetes diagnosis, I was prescribed insulin and a handful of other drugs. But more than that, I was encouraged to eat healthier. Well, the good news was that this whole experience was exactly the sort of shocker I needed to finally get my oversized butt in gear. I began eating mostly plant based foods, though I had some eggs and dairy from time to time. Basically I was eating a keto diet, though I didn't call it that (and no, I am not advocating a keto diet. It has its good sides, but health is complicated and no one diet is universal). I began to slowly lose a little weight, though I was still about 160 pounds over where I should be. My blood sugar was normal for most of that time, and my doctors were actually impressed by how low my A1C was (that's a blood test they do to measure blood sugar over a longer period of time).

While all this was happening, I began to notice an interesting side effect. I had been in the process of writing my second book when I got the abscess. Up to that point, I had been struggling with consistently writing it. Despite everything I knew about habits, I just couldn't seem to get them to work. I would return from work every day exhausted, I would find myself distracted by literally everything and anything. Most of the time, all I wanted to do was lay on the couch and watch Netflix.

That started to change after my hospital visit.

It wasn't long before I realized that I was having an easier time getting up in the morning. It wasn't nearly as hard as it had been before. What's more, soon after waking I would find myself at my desk, almost as if I hadn't thought about going there. For the first time in my writing career, I was writing every day, consistently.

The habits I had attempted to form before this experience weren't wasted. I was still training my mind to write when I needed it to write. But it wasn't until getting out of the hospital that this work truly cemented itself.

I credit this to my health.

Most of us living the standard American diet (which is not limited to Americans), do not even realize the effect that these foods have on us. Added sugar and processed foods are particularly bad. It's no wonder that diabetes, heart disease, and many other physical and mental illnesses are statistically linked to our society's increasing reliance on these foods.

Now this is not a health book for authors, though I intend to write one of those some day. But it is a warning. If you are having trouble with your habits, you might want to consider improving your health. Let me briefly outline a few things to try.

First of all, do not focus on losing weight. This is not the goal that will help you. Instead, focus on health goals that affect the mind. If you're doing them properly, the weight will come off eventually if you have weight to lose. But even skinny people can suffer from mental problems like brain fog, a lack of willpower, or irritability, all of which can be improved by fixing your diet. These are symptoms that we don't often associate with the food we eat, but they are. And they are preventable.

Some of the best ways to reduce these symptoms and increase your abilities include the following:

- Eat a lot of vegetables.

- Eat low-carb foods like lean meats and cheeses. Our society has long demonized these foods, and they certainly shouldn't be eaten more than vegetables and fruits, but they are also highly satiating, will prevent cravings, and do not have the same inhibiting effect on your mind. Fat is not the enemy as much as carbs are (carbs aren't the enemy either as long as they come from unprocessed foods).

- Be moderate in all things. There is no major food group that you necessarily want to eliminate completely, unless you have a specific, physical need to do so, with one, possibly two exceptions I get into below.

- Take a morning walk. Notice I didn't say exercise your butt off. Intense exercise is good, but one of the best ways to awaken your mind is to just take a simple walk, preferably in the morning. Bonus points if you're out in nature.

- Eliminate all added sugar and processed foods. This is the one major extreme that I cannot recommend enough. The obesity epidemic started with the rise of processed foods. Not before. There is no situation where even a moderate amount of added sugar or processed foods is good for you. It will always pull you back and keep you from your full potential. Always.

- Eliminate alcohol, or at least try to avoid it as much as possible. Our society makes this very difficult, but just as I said above for added sugar and processed foods, there is never a time when alcohol will help your body. Ever. Recent studies confirm this. All the added benefits we thought came from a small glass of wine actually has nothing to do with the alcohol content, but with the grape juice itself. Best to avoid if possible.

As I mentioned, I am not a health professional (yet), but I do read a lot of health professionals, and I have my own personal experience putting into practice the above tips. They work. But seeing as everyone is different, please consult your doctor before making any major changes, except for the added sugar and processed foods bit. Like I said, there's no universe where those do you any good, no matter who you are or what your body type is.

There aren't too many authors who talk about this much (with the exception of Joanna Penn and Euan Lawson in *The Healthy Writer*), but I think it's one of the most crucial parts of being a successful writer. All of the many plagues a writer has to deal with, from burnout to forming writer habits, to writer's block, can all be significantly improved by nothing else than eating healthily. I cannot overstate just how much our diet and activity levels affect our mental capacity. If you want to be at full strength, you must optimize your health.

What About AI?

There's one other aspect of efficient writing that I haven't mentioned yet, and that is using AI to write a book.

Now, I've written an entire book on the subject of *how* to write a book with AI, so I won't get into too much detail here. Basically, I think it's a great tool that can easily help authors who deal with some of the preexisting conditions that I've mentioned above like depression, ADHD, etc.

However, I do think that AI involves a different set of skills, most notably a lot of editing to get the quality up. I've noticed that many authors who are just starting out, and who haven't written a book before, don't actually know a lot about what makes a book good or bad, which makes it difficult to improve upon the AI-written material.

And so I stand by my early statement that you should be writing regularly, and I don't mean writing with AI. The good news is that if you are writing your main book with AI, you can spend your *actual* writing time on other things, like writing prompts and creative writing exercises. Focusing on those forms of deliberate practice will actually increase your writing skills faster than just writing the book without AI.

But my point is, I do think there are some skills to be gained that you can *only* get with experience writing on your own. For some, this will be difficult, but I still recommend it.

That said, I know there will be authors who, whether it be for time or for mental illness or something else, will not spend a lot of time actually writing, and will instead rely on AI for a lot of the grunt work. To you I simply recommend doing your best. You will still improve as an author by trying to improve the output that the AI gives you.

But understand that editing existing text is a different skill set than writing your own. That's not a bad thing, it's just different. And I still believe that the best way to improve writing is to write. But AI does provide some alternatives for those in unique circumstances, which is one of the great things about it.

Plus, there are a heap of advantages that AI gives you that don't involve writing the text for you. For those, I recommend every author go to town and use it to your heart's content. It will help a ton with decision fatigue, burnout, and writer's block. Combine that with the two principles of habits and health above, and you'll be golden.

10

Editing/Outlining

Alright, so let's talk about the two biggest tasks an author faces besides the actual writing: outlining and editing.

This is one of those areas where I'm going to bring up the 80/20 rule again, because it applies. In my experience, most authors prefer one or the other of these two tasks. I, for one, quite enjoy the outlining process, but rather detest editing. I know some authors who thrive in the editing process, but really hate outlining.

I mentioned earlier that outlining was essential if you want to be a financially successful author, because it helps tremendously with writing speed. That is still true. But the degree to which you outline can be a spectrum as well. An outline can be as simple as knowing where the book starts out, and where it will end, with everything in the middle as some other great discovery adventure. But the less detailed your outline, the more time it will take to write the book. I suppose you will also spend less time working on the outline, but chances are a generic outline will still slow you down overall.

That's not necessarily a bad thing. But here's the main side-effect of having a less detailed outline: you will need to edit a lot.

What you will need to edit can range dramatically, everything from adding a new character, to changing a setting because you didn't detail it well enough in your outline. But in my experience, and the same is true of other authors I've talked to, the less I outline, the more work will be left for me in the edit.

If you're one of those people that loves the editing process, than perhaps this approach is for you! It won't matter if your outline is simple, you would much prefer to fix it after the book has been written. If this is you, then go ahead!

For other authors like me, you might hate editing. Now I will say that you will need to do some editing (especially if you use AI), you can't get around it. But the degree at which you need to edit can depend a lot on your outline. If you have a really good outline, your editing needs will be minimal.

Here's my process. I'm a pretty thorough outliner. I go through three passes on my outline, fleshing it out every time. The first is just a general overview of what events need to happen, what the theme is, what the character needs to learn, etc. My next pass goes through all the major plot points, with at least a single sentence for each beat of the story. My third pass is where I flesh out character backgrounds/motivations, the descriptions of places that I'm going to visit, the collection of reference images to help with those descriptions, research on things like armor, weapons, etc. (remember I'm a fantasy writer, but most genres will have a similar degree of research needed). By this time, I may need to go back and tweak my plot outline to fit with a few things I learned in the third pass. But that's the general process overall. By the time I'm finished, I already have a good idea of who my characters are, what's going to happen to them, what every piece of their journey looks like, and so on.

Then I write my book, obviously. Because I've already developed a clear guide, this usually won't take me very long. In fact, while writing involves the most work, it's also the simplest step of this process.

When I'm done, I do one read through. This allows me to catch a few aspects that don't work, maybe minor plot holes, awkward sentences, and areas where I maybe didn't explain a character's thought process or the description of a setting well enough. Then I send it to my beta readers. They give me some notes, most of which are perfectly valid. But these changes do not take long to fix. If you've done your outlining well, you will mostly avoid many of the pitfalls in logic that beta readers are there to identify.

Sometimes, if I'm feeling up to it, I will read it through again at this point, just to make sure that the changes I made still fit with the overall story. But usually I send it to a proofreader to catch typos, grammar issues, and spelling mistakes. But that's it!

Occasionally, if I'm doing the first book in a series, I will spend a little extra time and money on more editors, particularly a developmental editor who will help me out with the story. But once again, if you're doing your outline well, your needs here will be minimal. However, if this is your first book, I highly recommend a developmental editor, and make sure they're good. You will learn SO MUCH from them, and that's the real value of developmental editors. They're teachers.

The reason I do this for the first book in the series is because it's the book that sells the rest of the series. If people don't like it, they will not continue reading and you'll sell fewer books. So it's worth spending a little extra time and money on this. This goes for pantsers too. Since the first book is crucial to get a proper read through of your series, the 80/20 rule suggests that it's where you should put more of your effort. Once a reader has read through the second book, they're more likely to be committed to your entire series. Drop off from book two to three is always much less than from book one to two. Unless your second book is a real mess.

So what's the bottom line here? Chances are, you enjoy either outlining or editing more than the other. If that's the case, I encourage you to put most of your effort into that thing, and not the other. You will still need to do some of both, but focusing strongly on one will exclude your need to focus just as strongly as the other. Remember, we're in the business of being efficient with our time here, so don't overwork yourself. You can still write a good book without much of an outline, or without much of an edit, but you MUST focus on at least one of these for it to work well.

Chapter 11
Improving Craft

I haven't talked about craft much in this book, and indeed, many self-published authors are a little hesitant to talk about it, since we focus a lot more on the business side of things. The business side is fine, but as the market becomes increasingly saturated with more and more indie authors doing all the same things that we are, or using AI to write books, we're going to need to stand out. After all, the books that go viral and keep selling even after years and years of being on the market are (usually) really well-written books.

There's no way to do this better than improving your craft. "Craft" is a blanket term authors often use to refer to the skill of telling a good story. The better your craft, the better your book and the better your characters are written. It's the creative part of a book business.

As I said, we don't often talk about it as much as we should in indie circles. I think this is partially due to imposter syndrome. We may know the business side of things (which is also easier to quantify), but to claim that we are equally good at craft seems like a much more conceited and overly proud claim.

I suffer from this, and though I probably do have a few good words of craft advice to give first-time authors, I'm uncomfortable even trying, because I'm also learning more and more. But I can give some advice to *improve* your craft.

I mentioned earlier that your first book is not likely to be very good, and I stand by that. It might not be *that* bad, but it will pale in comparison to the books you write even shortly thereafter. That is why my first piece of advice to improve your craft is to write, and do not stop writing. Use the advice I've given so far to establish a writing habit every day, and then write...all...the...time. Practice, after all, makes perfect.

But that being said, if all you're doing is writing the same sort of thing over and over, and not making a conscious effort to improve, your skill is likely to wane. So you must be making the effort to improve. I recommend doing this with some of the following three techniques:

1. Hire a developmental editor to review your book with you. Their personalized insight will give you a lot of ideas on where YOU, specifically, need to improve.

2. Read a book on craft and practice that specific skill in your next book. I don't recommend reading too many books at once and trying to incorporate all of that into your next book. It's too much to handle. Read one book, study one topic, and write a book with that improvement as your focus, then do the same for your next book. Over time, your books will get much better.

3. Read some other really good books in your genre and take notes. Incorporate what you learn into your future writings.

That last point is a favorite of mine. I'd much rather be analyzing stuff that I already know is successful than reading books with people telling me what to do. Maybe it's because I'm rebellious at heart and a secret part of my brain will want to do the opposite of what I'm told is "right" but I prefer hands-on learning.

Now, that could just be my style. If one of these other methods work better for you, by all means take them. But personally, I prefer actively reading other successful books and taking what I learn into my own writing.

This technique is also really good for learning how to write to market. In fact, this exercise is a lot like how to learn to write a good blurb using the templates I shared earlier. For example, let's say you want to write a military fantasy. You could start out by selecting 4-5 different military fantasy books, preferably newer bestsellers. Being a bestseller is important, because you're trying to learn how to replicate their success. As you read, mark down the different scenes. Point out what happens in that scene, which characters were involved (and their role in the story), as well as how that scene makes you feel. What is its purpose?

I call this the **Story Hacker Method** (hence the name of this series), analyzing the bestsellers in any genre for structure, character, and other things they might be getting right.

As you do this, you will begin to see trends in the different books of the same genre. You might even seen scenes matching up as if both had drawn from the same template. This doesn't mean that they aren't original. It just means that they follow a similar story structure. Two scenes might be totally different in the details, yet still serve the same purpose in the story.

There's one other technique that I really like to do, when combined with this genre analysis. It's called Copywork.

Copywork is basically the act of writing out the text of another book **by hand**. It's important to do this by hand.

Why?

Because there's something different that happens in your brain when you write something out by hand. It engages more areas of your brain, and as a result, you are more likely to absorb what you write more, and over time you will begin to improve your prose.

I do this with Brandon Sanderson's prose all the time, because he is my favorite author, and I'm genuinely in awe of how he writes, not just from a global, story structure and worldbuilding perspective, but on a paragraph by paragraph level.

And as I want to be more like him, I make sure copywork is a part of my strategy.

For those of you who read my book on AI, this is almost exactly like training *yourself* on a dataset of writing, rather than training the AI on a book.

In the end, there is really one superior way to improve your craft: write. Learning from books or examples is all well and good. But if you're not writing, none of that will matter. It's one thing to know the theory of how good stories are put together, and another entirely to actually put that into practice.

Writing, like playing the piano or learning how to draw, is a skill that takes time and steady practice to perfect. We've all heard that it takes 10,000 hours to become an expert at a skill. I don't know if I'd say it's that much, but it certainly does take a long time. If you don't start now, you'll never get there. Start writing today, and do not stop. That is ultimately the most important thing you can do. If you're diligent, the learning will come.

Step 4: Self-publishing

MYTHHQ

Myth HQ, LLC

12

CHOOSING A BOOK COVER

Alright, so at this point, I'm assuming you've finished the book and it's gone through some edits. Congratulations! Now it's time to start getting into the next step of actually publishing your book. And the first, and most important, asset we're going to talk about is the book cover.

Now, if you're following this guide exactly as I'm mapping it out, then you've already finished your book and are just now getting to the book cover.

I, however, create my book cover usually while I'm writing the book. Here's why:

The book cover is one of your most valuable pieces for marketing. It sets the tone for the entire book, and if that tone is off, it will manifest itself when your readers go through the book. They will quickly realize that the content of your book does not match the cover. This is why it's important to both write your book to market *and* create a cover that appeals to that same market.

It's also why I like to buy my covers before I've finished the book. Sometimes, I'll even buy the cover before I start writing it (but usually after I've done the outline). Because it not only sets the tone for your reader, it sets the tone for you as well.

When I was writing my first book, I'll admit I didn't have a clear idea of how the main character should act. At first, I wrote her as headstrong, perhaps a little prone to anger, and relying a little too much on the "powerful woman" trope. But what I really wanted was to show the progression of my character from being kind of timid and weak, to being one of the most powerful heroes this fantasy land would ever see. I managed to communicate this to the cover designer, and while I was part-way through the book, she sent me back her initial designs. The cover showed a girl in armor, but a girl who was also extremely young and innocent looking.

I immediately knew that the girl on the cover was the girl I wanted in my book. But the way she looked did not quite match up with how I was writing her. I was writing a bit more on the "wild woman" side, and less on the innocent, inexperienced side.

What I then did was I went back to the beginning and changed the character, before moving on to write her in the new style for the rest of the book. That book cover literally changed the way I wrote that book. It took some time (and I hate wasting time) so now I usually get the covers before I start writing. That gives me a clear tone to work from, and it helps my writing match the genre just a little better.

Why is a book cover so important? Because despite any axioms out there, everyone (and I mean everyone) *does* judge a book by its cover. It is the first thing that will grab a reader's attention, and it must do that job so well that it won't only spark interest, but create a burning desire in your reader's mind to read that book. The better you can do this, the better your books will sell. It doesn't matter how good your ads are, if you have a rotten book cover, you will never sell books.

The best way to identify what is and isn't a good book cover, is to go into a list of Amazon's bestsellers, or wander the isle of your local book store, and look at the books in your genre. Get a feel for the similarities these books have to each other. Over time, you'll be able to pick up trends, and your ability to correctly identify the market of any given genre will improve.

When I was first starting out, I didn't really have a clear idea of the difference between YA fantasy and Urban fantasy, at least when it came to book covers. I remember selecting an Urban Fantasy cover as an example of what I wanted part of my first cover to look like. Thankfully, my designer knew full well that Urban Fantasy was not what I was looking for, and wisely left that part out of the final design. Now I can tell you that Urban Fantasies almost always have a woman in a position of power, sometimes with a city as the background, but almost always with swirly magic colors surrounding them. Most also have a lot of darker colors to contrast with all the magic stuff floating around.

Because book covers are so important, this is one area that I recommend not penny pinching. If it requires a lot of money to get the best possible cover, then spend it. However, that doesn't mean you shouldn't still be smart with your money. My best recommendation is to do a search on Facebook for book cover artists. Look through the results and try to find some groups or pages of artists that do really good work, but don't yet have a huge following on Facebook (at least under 1,000 page likes or group members). There are also options out there like Miblart, which is my favorite low-budget design agency. There's also services like 99Designs, but know if you take that route, you will be spending a lot more money than necessary. The advantage to 99Designs is that you get to look at a lot of different options and choose which one you like best, but the prices are enormous. I spent $500 for my first cover (which I did through 99Designs), and I later found out that my designer does custom book covers for $230. So if I had gone to that artist directly, I could have saved a lot of money.

For my second series, I sought out a new designer directly and took a leap of faith by hiring them because I liked their work and their prices were very reasonable. If your designer understands the genre well, it's okay even if they don't quite get your vision right. The book will still sell because they were able to appeal to the correct market. And you will likely save money in the meantime.

Many artists also have the option of buying pre-made book covers that, as the name suggests, are already available. These tend to be a little more generic, but may still appeal to the right genre. In fact, many of these pre-made book covers appeal to the genre better than custom covers. This is particularly true of romance.

Whatever you do, make sure you're hitting the correct market, and that it matches the genre of your book. The best way to get bad reviews is to have a book cover that promises one genre, but have your actual book be of another genre, even if it's only slightly different. You see, most people who leave bad reviews didn't do so because they thought your book was genuinely bad. Most do so because you violated a trope of the genre they tend to like reading. This is especially true if your cover gives the wrong impression. So make sure you get this part right. Apart from writing the actual book, the book cover is the most important step forward toward making a living as an author.

13

WRITING THE BLURB

Second to the book cover, but also very important, is your book blurb. Most readers, when they're looking at your book, will go through a conversion funnel that goes something like this: They see your book cover, they're interested so they click to learn more, then they read your book blurb to see if it sounds like an interesting story.

Now that could be enough to get them to click the big "Buy" button, though some readers will go a step further and open up the preview to read the first few paragraphs (side note: make sure your first few pages are the best pages in the book), but what we really want is for the blurb to be the thing that sells your book. The cover starts the process, but the blurb is what should finish it (with the preview as a backup).

The definitive book on this subject is Bryan Cohen's *How to Write a Sizzling Synopsis*. Bryan owns a whole company with the sole purpose to write book blurbs for authors, so he knows what he's talking about. I'm not going to get into much detail here, except to offer one suggestion (assuming you don't have the money to pay someone like Bryan for a book description). Read his book and you'll have a better understanding of how it works. But in addition to that, here's my method that has worked rather well for me in the past:

Go back to the bestsellers list on Amazon. Select 3-5 of the top selling books in your genre. You can pick tradition-ally-published books, but I would actually recommend that most of your selections be indie-published. Traditional pub-lishers don't always feel the need to tweak and tighten their blurbs because they have more money to back them up. We indies need all the help we can get, and we're always refining and improving. That means that if you see an indie title in the top 20 in your genre, they're probably doing something right with their blurb.

Once you have your selections, go through each blurb sen-tence by sentence to see what it's doing. Write out what role each sentence is playing, like "Protagonist lives a normal life, until there's an inciting incident that throws her world upside down." or "The protagonist meets the love interest who she does not like, but they are forced to work together." Here's a specific example of a blurb for A Kingdom of Exiles as well as my analysis version:

Original Blurb:

The brightest of stars are always born on the darkest of nights. Serena Smith is unusual.

Growing up in a backwoods village, her life is lonely and dull. Then, on her eighteenth birthday, she's gifted a magical heirloom only to be snatched by fae and condemned to a lifetime in chains.

Dragged to Aldar, a fae kingdom ruled by a tyrant witch, Serena discovers a forbidden love, and meets fellow outcasts, each with their own dark secrets.

As the lives of warriors, rebels, and witches clash,they find a shared destiny. For only together, and with Serena's unique gifts, can they survive long enough to build the flames of a revolution. Only together can they go to war ...

From the author of Draken comes this explosive new fantasy series with lots of heart and a sting in its tail.

What are you waiting for? Scroll up and one-click now to find out why readers all over the world have fallen in love with A Kingdom of Exiles!

My Analysis:

Teaser, suggesting darkness within, 12 words.

Reveal of main character and what sets her apart.

Statement of place where main character is coming from, the norm. Inciting event, character thrust out of comfort zone.

New situation, reveal of dark setting, allies/romance, and the mystery surrounding them.

Statement of finding new purpose with said allies. Statement of how the main character's uniqueness contributes to new purpose. Explanation of the stakes.

Once you have this analysis for several blurbs, you'll begin to note some similarities between them. You can then begin to construct your own blurb based on these structures you've set up. I like to create one master structure that combines all the different analyses of the blurbs, then write my own blurb based on that. It's a great way to create a blurb that works for your genre without shelling out a lot of money for one.

Additionally, if you use AI to help, using this method will give you a framework that makes the output from the AI all that much better. So this is definitely a practice I recommend you do.

14

HAVE AN EXPERIMENT LOSS-LEADER

Alright, here is another tip I have specifically for first-time authors that I don't always see other authors talk about: have a book to experiment on. Put simply, this is a short book, novella, or short story that you can afford to experiment with, and maybe even lose money on.

Now let me clarify: you don't have to do this if you're doing the book-splitting method I talked about in a previous chapter. If you've already written a book and split it into 4 novellas, then you'll get a lot of experience just from publishing those, and a loss-leader won't really be necessary. Although if you want to use it, it can still help. It's just more work that I think is unnecessary if you're already splitting your book.

But if you're not doing the splitting method, it can be a beneficial tactic to have an experimental loss-leader. Why?

I've found this to be a really great way for a first-time author to learn the ropes. Having a book that you don't plan to make any money on is a great way to stretch your publishing muscles and become familiar with some of the techniques we use *before* you actually publish your first series.

You see, when you publish your first series, you want it to be good. You want to knock it out of the water. The problem is that, for many authors, this is also the first time they've uploaded a book to Kindle Direct Publishing (KDP), or the first time they've run ads, or even the first time that they've sent out an email. There are a lot of firsts happening, and it pays to get a little practice before that happens. You would be amazed by how much you learn just by going through the KDP uploading process, not to mention all the other things that happen when you first publish a book.

Your experimental book will help you get past all that. It will give you a chance to know what you're doing before you publish your main series, and that will help your series succeed.

For me, the experiment was that superhero-time-travel-urban-fantasy-science-fiction serial that I've mentioned several times now. And as much of a train wreck as that was, I wouldn't change anything about the role it served in helping me learn. It was absolutely essential, not for its own merit, but for what it taught me before I published my first series.

I took that book and uploaded it to KDP, I ran a few advertising dollars on it to see how that worked, I submitted it to a couple of promotions, and overall it simply helped me understand how this whole self-publishing thing worked.

By the time I actually published my first series, I knew a lot more about publishing, advertising, newsletters, promotions, etc. because I had published this serial ahead of time. My first series launch was highly improved because of that.

I've since taken the serial off of Amazon (at least the ebook version) and now my newsletter subscribers can get it for free. This is what I recommend for those using their reader magnet as their experimental loss-leader.

If you decide to use your reader magnet in this role, I wouldn't make it permanently listed on Amazon or any other retailer. Go ahead and upload it, run some advertising on it, see what you can learn. But when you're done, I would take it off Amazon. Here's why:

Every time someone buys your reader magnet on Amazon, they are most likely not subscribing to your email newsletter, which means that the primary purpose of that reader magnet is being circumvented. You don't want that short story or whatever it is to be available elsewhere. It must be an exclusive to your newsletter, or many people won't bother to sign up to get it.

So go ahead and experiment with it, but eventually I recommend you take it off and use it exclusively for your newsletter. In my case, I did both. I had a reader magnet that was exclusive to my newsletter, and I put the serial collection up on Amazon. Of course, I would later take it off Amazon and add it to the many things people could get by signing up for my newsletter, thereby adding value to that email list. I will soon begin re-writing the story from that serial as a proper book series, and since my newsletter has been exposed to the story before, I imagine that will help build a lot of hype for that upcoming series.

The bottom line is this: don't try to launch your first series without experimenting first. You might lose a few advertising dollars on something that you don't, ultimately, intend to sell, but it will be worth it to you in the long run.

15

FORMATTING YOUR BOOK

I 'm going to be honest here, formatting is a huge topic that anyone could spend a whole book talking about. There's so much to it, and it's all-too-often ignored by authors, at their expense.

A poorly formatted book leaves a very bad taste in a reader's mouth. You definitely want to make sure you format your manuscript before you publish. But since it's such a complex topic, I've chosen to make my recommendation simple: just go with Atticus.

Atticus is a formatting tool that is cloud based, so it works on Windows, Mac, Linux, Chromebook, etc.

It's not the only formatting tool out there. For instance, there's another called Vellum that is almost as good, but it's Mac only, and it costs $100 more than Atticus. And then there's Adobe InDesign, but that one is far MORE than what most of us need, and I really only recommend it if you do out-of-the-ordinary publications, like magazines or comic books.

But for the rest of us, Atticus is a fantastic formatting tool, and it's the only tool that I could almost call required for any aspiring author.

So let's briefly break down how to format your book in Atticus, and what to watch out for:

Setting Up Your Book Project

The first step to create your book project in Atticus is straightforward. This is where you'll input basic information about your book, such as the title and author name.

Entering Detailed Book Information

Next, you'll dive deeper into your book's metadata such as subtitle and publisher. Bear in mind that some of this information shows up in the title page of your book, so you want to make sure it accurately reflects the book you're trying to create.

Getting Your Manuscript into Atticus

This step is about transferring your words into the Atticus system. Whether you're writing directly in Atticus or uploading an existing manuscript, the goal is the same: to get your content into a format that Atticus can work with.

Note that every book is divided into three sections: front matter, body, and back matter. Atticus has templates for any type of content that belongs in one of these three sections, from copyright acknowledgements to full-page images to the About the Author page.

There are also a lot of formatting options that you have within the text editor itself. There's the regular bolding and italics, but a lot more options as well, including things like adding images, formatting quotes and verse, adding sub-headings, ornamental breaks, and even footnotes/endnotes.

Choosing and Customizing Your Book's Theme

This is where the magic happens. Choosing a theme is about giving your book its unique look and feel. It's not just about aesthetics - it's about meeting genre expectations and creating a cohesive reading experience.

Atticus has a lot of different templates to choose from, and just using those templates might be enough. But if you want, you can customize virtually every single element of these templates, from the images used, to the font and sizes of your title. Literally everything can be tweaked.

Strategically, this step is about branding. Your book's theme should align with your genre and appeal to your target audience. It should also be consistent with your author brand if you plan to write multiple books. I always use the exact same template for each book in a series, for example.

Exporting Your Formatted Book

The final step is getting your beautifully formatted book out of Atticus and ready for publication. This is where you'll create the files you'll upload to retailers.

There are three files that Atticus exports to:

- DOCX: this is mostly just to share with editors and other people who need a look at an early version of your book

- EPUB: this is the most common ebook format, and what you are likely to use when uploading to Amazon and other retailers

- PDF: this is the version you'll want to use for any print copies of your book. It's formatted to include things like the gutter margin, and comes in a variety of trim sizes designed for KDP or IngramSpark.

So I know that may feel like a lot, but don't worry, it's actually not that hard at all once you've done it once, especially if you've used Atticus. Once you've got your settings that you like, every book after that becomes just a few clicks to get it where it needs to be.

16

SELECTING YOUR KEYWORDS

I used to work at Kindlepreneur, and Dave Chesson is *the guy* when it comes to finding your keywords. You see, when you upload your book to Amazon, you're going to need seven keywords to help the discoverability of your book on Amazon.

So with that in mind, here are some steps to understand and choose the right keywords. I'm giving you the long answer here, but I also recommend Publisher Rocket to make some of these processes much easier.

Before we delve into the strategies for selecting the best keywords, let's first understand what Amazon KDP keywords are and why they're so crucial to your book's success.

What Are Amazon KDP Keywords?

Amazon KDP keywords are the words or phrases that you input when publishing your book through Kindle Direct Publishing. These keywords help Amazon's search algorithm understand what your book is about and determine when to show it in search results.

When a potential reader types a query into Amazon's search bar, the algorithm scans through millions of products, including books, to find the most relevant matches. Your keywords play a significant role in this process, acting as signposts that guide readers to your book.

The 7 Kindle Keyword Boxes

When you're setting up your book on KDP, you'll encounter seven boxes where you can input your keywords. Each box allows up to 50 characters, giving you a total of 350 characters to work with. But how should you approach filling these boxes? Should you aim for quantity, cramming in as many keywords as possible, or focus on quality with a few targeted phrases?

From what I learned when working for Kindlepreneur, the answer is a balance of both.

The Quantity Approach

Filling all 50 characters in each box with multiple keywords or phrases can increase the number of search terms for which your book is indexed. This means your book has the potential to appear in more search results, increasing its overall visibility.

For example, instead of just using "fantasy" in one box, you might use "fantasy magic dragons elves sorcery" to cover more ground.

The Quality Approach

On the other hand, using specific, targeted phrases can improve your book's ranking for those particular terms. This means that while your book might appear in fewer search results, it's more likely to rank higher in the ones it does appear in.

For instance, using "epic fantasy adventure" as a single keyword phrase could help you rank better for that specific term.

The Balanced Strategy

The research suggests that the most effective approach is a combination of both strategies. Here's how to implement it:

1. **Use 1-3 boxes for specific, targeted phrases**: These should be highly relevant to your book and have a good balance of search volume and competition.

2. **Use 1-2 boxes for category-specific keywords**: This helps reinforce your category choices and could potentially get your book into additional relevant categories.

3. **Fill the remaining boxes with niche-specific terms**: Use a mix of broad and specific terms related to your book's genre, themes, and content.

Let's break this down further.

Step 1: Identify 1-3 Specific Keyword Phrases

These are your power keywords. They should be:

1. **Highly relevant to your book**: Think about what your ideal reader would type into Amazon when looking for a book like yours.

2. **Have search volume**: Use a tool like Publisher Rocket to check how many people are searching for these terms monthly.

3. **Not overly competitive**: Again, Publisher Rocket's competition score can help you gauge this. Aim for keywords with a good balance of search volume and low competition.

Examples:

- For a weight loss book: "how to lose weight fast"

- For a fantasy novel: "epic fantasy adventure"

- For a productivity book: "time management for entrepreneurs"

Step 2: Select 1-2 Category-Specific Keywords

This step is crucial for reinforcing your category choices and potentially getting into additional relevant categories. Here's how to do it:

1. Use Publisher Rocket's category search feature to find relevant categories for your book.

2. Click on the "keywords" button for your chosen categories to see a list of related keywords.

3. Select 1-2 of these keywords or combine them to create keyword phrases that fit your book.

For example, if your book fits in the "Books > Science Fiction & Fantasy > Fantasy > Epic" category, you might use keywords like "epic fantasy series" or "fantasy quest adventure".

Step 3: Fill Remaining Boxes with Niche-Specific Terms

For the remaining keyword boxes, aim to fill as much of the 50-character limit as possible with terms relevant to your book's niche. This helps you cast a wider net while still staying relevant.

For fiction, consider words that describe:

- Your characters or their roles

- The setting and time period

- The central conflict or catalyst of your story

- Your specific sub-genre

For non-fiction, think about:

- The pain points your book addresses

- The benefits or outcomes readers can expect

- Your target audience demographics

- Key concepts or methodologies you cover

Example for a fantasy novel: "dragon rider magic quest prophecy medieval"

Example for a productivity book: "time management productivity hacks work-life balance"

Advanced Keyword Strategies

Now that we've covered the basics, let's dive into some advanced strategies to maximize the effectiveness of your keywords.

Leverage Amazon's Search Algorithm

Amazon's search algorithm is sophisticated and can understand variations of your keywords. Here's what you need to know:

1. **Word order doesn't matter**: Amazon will index your book for all combinations of the words you use. For example, "cozy mystery bakery" will also index for "mystery cozy bakery", "bakery cozy", "mystery bakery", etc.

2. **Plurals are automatic**: You don't need to include both singular and plural forms of a word. Amazon does this automatically.

3. **Quotation marks are unnecessary**: Don't use quotation marks around your phrases. This limits your indexing to that exact phrase only.

Avoid Keyword Stuffing

While it's tempting to repeat important keywords, Amazon advises against this practice. Repeating keywords doesn't appear to improve your ranking and could potentially harm it. Use each valuable keyword only once, making the most of your limited character space.

Leverage Your Title and Subtitle

Having a keyword in your title or subtitle can improve your ranking for that term by up to 37% compared to having it in the keyword fields alone. While you shouldn't stuff your title with keywords, including one or two important ones can significantly boost your visibility.

Update Your Keywords Regularly

The Amazon marketplace is dynamic, with new books being published and reader interests shifting constantly. Regularly updating your keywords (every 3-6 months) can help maintain and improve your book's visibility over time.

Common Keyword Mistakes to Avoid

Even with the best intentions, authors often make mistakes when selecting their keywords. Here are some pitfalls to watch out for:

1. **Using irrelevant keywords**: Don't use keywords that aren't truly relevant to your book, even if they're popular. Amazon's algorithm is smart enough to recognize this, and it could hurt your book's visibility.

2. **Ignoring long-tail keywords**: Long-tail keywords (phrases of 3+ words) often have less competition and can be highly effective.

3. **Using subjective terms**: Avoid using subjective descriptors like "best" or "great" in your keywords. Amazon doesn't allow these.

4. **Including competitor names or book titles**: This is against Amazon's guidelines and can get your book removed from the store.

5. **Neglecting to research**: Don't guess at what keywords might work. Use tools like Publisher Rocket to research actual search volumes and competition levels.

6. **Using temporary keywords**: Avoid using timely terms like "new release" or "on sale now" in your keywords, as these will quickly become outdated.

7. **Ignoring your target audience**: Make sure your keywords reflect the language and search terms your ideal readers would actually use.

And if all of that was a bit confusing for you, don't worry. Publisher Rocket is definitely the tool I recommend to make this whole process easier. Additionally, Dave Chesson has several amazing articles on his website that dig even deeper, so I'd check those out.

17

Selecting Your Categories

When you publish on KDP, one of the most crucial decisions you'll make is selecting the right categories for your book. You only get three, and you want to make sure that all three count.

Getting the Coveted Orange "Bestseller" Tag

We love to see the orange bestseller tag, a little tag at the top of a book that shows if it's a #1 bestseller in a particular Amazon category. It's not just fun for you, but you can use it as a marketing tool as well. But how do you get one?

The key lies in understanding Amazon's bestseller lists. Each category on Amazon has its own bestseller list, and if your book ranks #1 in any category, it earns the "Bestseller" tag. This tag appears not only on your book's product page but also in search results, making it a powerful attractor for potential readers.

However, it's important to note that being a "bestseller" on Amazon doesn't necessarily mean you're outselling every other book on the platform. It simply means you're the top seller in at least one specific category. This is where strategic category selection becomes crucial.

The Power of Niche Categories

While it might seem counterintuitive, aiming for a niche category can often be more beneficial than targeting a broad, highly competitive one. For instance, ranking #1 in "Books > Mystery, Thriller & Suspense > Thrillers & Suspense > Supernatural > Werewolves & Shifters" is much easier than topping the overall "Mystery, Thriller & Suspense" category. Yet, you'll still earn that "Bestseller" tag, which applies across Amazon.

This strategy allows you to leverage the prestige of being a "bestseller" while competing in a less crowded space. It's about finding that sweet spot where your book's topic aligns with a category specific enough to be attainable, yet broad enough to attract a significant audience.

Now don't get me wrong, we want to make sure these categories are relevant too. And I always make sure that one of my three categories is always the most relevant, even if the category itself is still super saturated and difficult to rank in.

But regardless, it's still nice to find at least two other categories that are super relevant, but also low competition so you can gain that added visibility (and if all goes well, the orange bestseller tag).

So let's dig into how to get there.

Analyzing ABSR (Amazon Best Sellers Rank)

To effectively choose your categories, you need to understand the Amazon Best Sellers Rank (ABSR). This is a number assigned to every product on Amazon, including books, that indicates how well it's selling compared to other products in its category.

The ABSR is updated hourly and takes into account recent and historical sales data. A lower number indicates better sales. For example, an ABSR of 1,000 means your book is the 1,000th best-selling item in its category on Amazon.

Your book's ABSR determines its ranking within each category it's listed in. The book with the lowest ABSR in a category ranks #1, the second-lowest ranks #2, and so on.

This means that to become a #1 bestseller in a category, your book needs to have a lower ABSR than any other book in that category. This is why analyzing the ABSR of current bestsellers in your target categories is crucial.

Let's say you're considering two categories for your book:

1. In Category A, the current #1 bestseller has an ABSR of 5,000.

2. In Category B, the #1 bestseller has an ABSR of 50,000.

To become the #1 bestseller in Category A, you'd need to sell enough books to achieve an ABSR lower than 5,000. For Category B, you'd only need to beat 50,000. Clearly, it would be easier to become a bestseller in Category B.

This doesn't mean you should always choose the easiest category to rank in. You need to balance the ease of ranking with the relevance and potential audience size of the category. A #1 rank in a tiny, obscure category might not drive as many sales as a #10 rank in a larger, more visible category.

Amazon's Old System

Before we dive into the current system, it's worth understanding how Amazon's category selection process used to work, as it provides context for the current approach and highlights why the new system is an improvement.

The BISAC System

In the past, when authors uploaded their books to KDP, they were presented with a list of BISAC (Book Industry Standards and Communications) categories. BISAC is a standard used by many in the publishing industry to categorize books by subject.

Authors would choose from this list, which was quite limited compared to the actual number of categories on Amazon. There were only about 4,000 BISAC categories to choose from, while Amazon actually has over 16,000 categories on their store.

This system created a disconnect between what authors could select during the publishing process and what actually appeared on Amazon. Amazon would take the BISAC selection and attempt to map it to their own category system, but this wasn't always accurate or optimal.

The "Secret" Categories

More savvy authors discovered that there were additional "secret" categories on Amazon that weren't available through the BISAC selection process. To get into these categories, authors had to contact Amazon directly and request to be placed in specific categories.

This created an uneven playing field, where authors who knew about this "trick" could potentially gain an advantage over those who didn't.

Amazon eventually created a form that authors could use to request category changes or additions. This allowed authors to be placed in up to 10 categories, far more than the initial two or three they could select during the publishing process.

While this was an improvement, it still required extra effort from authors and created a system where the most successful authors were often those who best understood these hidden mechanisms.

How to Choose Categories Now

In June 2023, Amazon made a significant change to their category selection process. They moved away from the BISAC system and now allow authors to choose directly from Amazon's own categories during the publishing process. This change has several important implications:

- **Direct Access to Amazon Categories:** Authors now have direct access to Amazon's full category structure. This means you can see and select from the actual categories your book will appear in on Amazon, rather than choosing a BISAC category and hoping Amazon maps it correctly.

- **More Specific Categories:** Amazon's category structure is more granular than the BISAC system, allowing for more specific categorization. This can help your book find its most relevant audience.

- **Limitation to Three Categories:** While authors previously could request up to 10 categories, Amazon now limits selection to three categories. This makes each choice more crucial and requires more strategic thinking.

- **No More Category Change Requests:** Amazon no longer accepts category change requests through their previous form system. All category selections must be made through the KDP dashboard.

How to Select Your Categories

1. Log into your KDP dashboard and go to your book's "Edit eBook Content" or "Edit Paperback Content" page.

2. Scroll down to the "Categories" section.

3. Click on "Add categories" to open the category selection tool.

4. Use the navigation to drill down into specific categories. You can select up to three.

5. Once you've made your selections, click "Save" to confirm your choices.

Remember, you're looking for categories that are:

- Relevant to your book's content

- Specific enough to be less competitive

- Popular enough to drive meaningful traffic

The Importance of Research

Before making your selections, it's crucial to research potential categories. Look at the bestsellers in each category you're considering. Ask yourself:

- How well is my book likely to compete here?

- Is this category truly relevant to my book's content?

- What ABSR do I need to hit to rank well in this category?

This research phase is where tools like Publisher Rocket can be invaluable, as we'll discuss in the next section.

How Publisher Rocket Will Make it Easier

While it's possible to do all the necessary category research manually, it can be a time-consuming and complex process. This is where a tool like Publisher Rocket comes in, significantly streamlining and enhancing your category selection process.

Here are a few features:

- **Comprehensive Category Database:** Publisher Rocket maintains a database of all 11,000+ Amazon book categories. This means you can explore every possible category option for your book, including those that might be hard to find through Amazon's interface alone.

- **ABSR Analysis:** For each category, Publisher Rocket

shows you the ABSR of the current #1 and #10 best-sellers. This information is crucial for understanding how competitive a category is and how many sales you'd need to rank well.

- **Sales Estimates:** Publisher Rocket can estimate how many books you'd need to sell per day to rank #1 or in the top 10 for each category. This helps you set realistic goals and choose categories where success is achievable.

- **Kindle Unlimited and Large Publisher Data**: The tool also shows you what percentage of the best-sellers in each category are enrolled in Kindle Unlimited or come from large publishers. This can help you make informed decisions about your publishing strategy.

- **Historical Data:** Publisher Rocket provides historical data for categories, allowing you to see trends over time. This can help you identify categories that are growing in popularity or becoming less competitive.

Choosing the RIGHT Categories

Now that we understand the tools at our disposal, let's dive into the strategy of choosing the right categories for your book. This process involves balancing several factors:

- Relevance: First and foremost, your chosen categories must be relevant to your book's content. Amazon may remove your book from categories they deem inappropriate, and more importantly, readers who find your book through an irrelevant category are likely to be disappointed, leading to poor reviews.

- Competitiveness: You want to choose categories where you have a realistic chance of ranking well. This usually means looking for niche categories that align with your book's specific subject matter.

- Visibility: While niche categories are often less competitive, you also need to ensure they have enough visibility to drive meaningful traffic to your book. Look for categories that have a good balance of specificity and popularity.

Amazon May Put You in More Categories (Or Take You Away)

It's important to understand that your category selections are not the final word on where your book appears on Amazon. Amazon's algorithms continuously analyze your book's content, keywords, and performance to determine the most appropriate categories.

And while you can only directly select three categories, Amazon may place your book in additional categories based on your keywords and book content. This is why it's crucial to use relevant keywords in your book title, subtitle, description, and keyword fields.

For example, if you've written a historical mystery set in Victorian London, you might use keywords like "Victorian era," "London detective," and "historical whodunit." These could help Amazon's algorithms categorize your book more accurately, potentially placing it in additional relevant categories beyond your initial three selections.

Conversely, Amazon may remove your book from categories if they determine it's not a good fit. This usually happens if:

1. Your book's content doesn't match the category.

2. Your book consistently underperforms in a category.

3. Readers report that your book is miscategorized.

This is why it's crucial to choose relevant categories from the start and ensure your book's content, title, description, and keywords accurately represent its genre and themes.

Once again, I recommend Publisher Rocket and the resources at Kindlepreneur if you want to dive deeper on this subject. But if you follow my guidance above, you should have what you need to get started.

But once you have your keywords and categories settled, as well as your book cover and book description, not to mention the actual manuscript itself, you'll have everything you need to publish your book on Amazon.

18

RAPID RELEASING

Alright, now we start to get to the fun stuff: your launch! You've written your book, set up your newsletter, bought your cover, written your blurb, and everything is ready to go!

And if you've done as I suggested and split your book into 3-4 novellas, you're even more ready for this next step. If you don't plan on splitting those books, you might want to wait until you have another book or two ready.

There's a common strategy in the indie publishing space at the moment, that of rapid release. Though it's unclear if this is universally true, it would seem that Amazon tends to favor authors who release books quickly. There is definitely evidence that your book will gain less and less exposure from Amazon over time, with what we call the "drops". The biggest of these happens at 30 days, when a book no longer appears on the "New Releases" list on Amazon. There's also evidence of a second drop at 60 days, and a third at 90 days. That is why many authors will choose to release their books at least 30 days apart. Some will even release them weeks apart.

Now, of course we're not asking you to write a book a month. That is, frankly, hard, even with AI assistance. And it's especially difficult when you're just starting out. However, if you would have a little patience, I might suggest that you wait until you have approximately three books ready to publish before your first book goes live. If you're splitting your book, then you're already there, if not, then you will need to write more. Here are a few reasons why:

Firstly, to be perfectly honest, readers don't really trust someone with only one book out. If all you have is one single novel, even if the cover and blurb are amazing, few people will trust you to provide them with an engaging experience. Readers are fishing for new worlds to dive into, new favorite authors, new universes. It's unlikely that you can become someone's favorite author if you only have one book, and a single novel is not nearly enough for a person to really dive in and lose themselves in your world. A single novel is a start, but some of these readers can really commit. If you don't have anything for them to commit to, they won't even give you the chance to impress them.

The second book is the best marketing of your first. But obviously, you have to start with only one, right? So what do you do during that time (however brief) when you only have one book? Well, if you want that book to sell, you need to at least give people notice that you will soon have other books. The best way to do this is to put your sequel(s) on preorder. Amazon allows you to have a book on preorder several months ahead of time. When you release your first book, I STRONGLY recommend you have the sequel available for preorder. I believe the ideal scenario is to have the first two sequels of your book available when your first book launches. Amazon allows you to create a series page for your book, so you can link all three, and people will see all three listed just under the blurb of each book. This will not only encourage sell-through of your series, but will help convince people to give it a chance in the first place.

Personally, I write almost the whole series before I'm ready to launch it. At least, that's how I do it now. When I launched my first series, my biggest mistake is that I launched the first few books quickly, but let the remainder lag.

I released my first proper book (not counting the serial) on July 31, 2018. My second book was released a week later, and the third was released two weeks after that. By the time my third book was out, that series had exploded in sales, totalling nearly a thousand by the end of the month. However, I made the big mistake of not continuing to write the fourth one fast enough to get it out right away. I should have put it on preorder and released it a month after the third book. But I waited. I didn't release it until five months after the third book. By then, the momentum that I had built up had completely died, and even several more books in the series could not revive it.

Had I been more prepared, and motivated myself to write those books and get them out right away, that launch could have been significantly more impactful. For future series, things will be different.

Now all of this is assuming you want a huge launch of your first series. In some cases, you might not want that. Even with a rapid release strategy, it's very hard to get your very first series to the point that it's making the big bucks. Everything will have to be on point, from your cover to your release strategy.

For many, becoming an author is a long game, and ultimately the slow accumulation of fans is the better strategy. And Amazon's algorithms could change so that rapid releases don't work as well. It's okay to put out some books and not make money at first. Just remember that all of this is leading up to success (once you have a lot of books out and have slowly built up a fanbase). None of it is a waste, even if your first book makes little to nothing.

A Note on Pre-orders

Pre-orders are a bit of a question mark among some authors. Some use them, some don't. Many will argue that the pre-orders can mildly mess up the algorithm. I'll talk a bit more about that algorithm in the next chapter, but for now let me just say that Amazon appears to count preorders as sales on the very first day, which could lead the algorithm to believe that you've had a fluke spike, and therefore refrain from marketing it on their own (which you want them to do).

On the other hand, preorders have other significant benefits. I've already talked about why it's important to have a second or third book listed when you launch your first book, if only to provide the reader with a promise that there's more coming.

Preorders also provide intense motivation for you to finish your book. If you miss a preorder, and you have to go into KDP and delay it so that your book comes out later than you originally marked, Amazon will penalize you for it. If you miss your preorder, you will not be able to preorder again for a full year. You don't want that to happen. Therefore, if I put a book up to release in, say, three months, I now have sufficient motivation to finish that book before the deadline. It's one of the best way to use deadlines to your advantage.

19

"Gaming" the System

Okay, let's talk briefly about algorithms. This is one of those areas that is constantly changing, and I'm not an expert by far. My first introduction to the topic was from Chris Fox, who wrote a whole book called *Six Figure Author: Using Data to Sell Books.*

But here are some of the big ideas simplified for you. Amazon's algorithm is highly refined to help connect their customers with products those customers will want to buy. Have you ever noticed a time when you've glanced at a product, and suddenly you start seeing that product or a bunch of related products popping up all over Amazon and even on other websites? That's because of Amazon's algorithm. It's one of the most sophisticated algorithms out there.

Algorithms used to be easy to game. We saw this in the early days of Google, where all you had to do was include a keyword you wanted to rank for a million times on your page, and it would come up first in the search results. That no longer happens, and these big algorithms are much harder to game now that people like Amazon and Google have had the time and thousands of man-hours to refine their process.

But it can be done, at least a little. And if you do it right, Amazon will begin to market *for* you. They will show your book to people who they know are the right type to buy your book. And that's exactly what you want to kick off when you launch your series. If you can get Amazon to do that, it's smooth sailing from there. Here are a couple of strategies:

- **Rapid releases:** We already talked about this in the last chapter. This is part of what may be an algorithm benefit, a technique that encourages Amazon to show your products to readers who are likely to buy them. It's not entirely clear if rapid releases alone encourage algorithm boosts, or if it's a combination of several things. But overall, those who have rapid releases tend to do better.

- **Showing your book to the right people:** One of the ways to "train" Amazon's algorithm is to make sure that the first people to buy your book are exactly the right type of people who would like that book. It's easy to think that you should get your book out in front of as many people as possible. The more sales the better, right? WRONG! Let's say that people of all different backgrounds and interests buy your book. All this does is confuse the algorithm. But if it can see a clear trend in the types of books your readers buy, it will begin marketing your book to others who match the same profile. This is why having a newsletter with people who read your genre is so important. They will help train the algorithm correctly. This is also why you should NOT try to market the book to your general friends and family. They are more likely to buy the book because they know you, not because they read those types of books, and this will only serve to confuse Amazon's algorithm.

- **The Curve:** There is some solid evidence to suggest that Amazon likes to see a slow curve of increased sales. To them, this is evidence of word of mouth building up, creating a snow-ball effect of sales. That is why you don't want to blast everyone with news about your book all at once. This is also why preorders are thought by some to be a bad idea, since Amazon counts your preorders as sales on the first day, which could throw off your slow curve. When I launch a series, I start with a moderate advertising budget and slowly increase it every day for the first 1-2 weeks. I also send out my emails to different sections of my newsletter, targeting the least engaged first, then the moderately engaged, then the most engaged. Because I know the most engaged members of my newsletter are the most likely to buy the book, so I'll likely get increasing sales as I segment the newsletter in this fashion.

Gaming the algorithm is one of those things that isn't guaranteed to work forever. Already, Amazon is more of a pay-to-play model, where in order to gain the kind of exposure they used to just give you, you now have to pay for advertising spots. Trends like this are likely to continue as competition increases.

Ultimately, the best thing you can do is ensure that you have an awesome book, and that it looks and sounds like an awesome book. If you can do that, over time these tricks will occur naturally, and you'll begin to make money the way any of us could ever hope to do.

Step 5: The Marketing

Myth HQ, LLC

20

MARKETING

So now that we've written our reader magnet, established our email list, written the book, and published it, it's finally time to start marketing.

Now in a way, the actions you take in Steps 1 and 2 are already starting the marketing ball rolling. But that's just to build your email list, which is one of the most important things you can do at the start. Now that you have a book or series of books released, it's time to crank up the marketing techniques.

I've worked in marketing for 12+ years, and let me just say that there are countless ways to market something, and they all vary in effectiveness depending on what your product is. We've already touched on email marketing and how that one is important. It still is, but there are many other avenues that businesses and corporations take for their marketing. Some of them are only possible because they have a lot of money to throw at those options. You could do anything from actively calling people to make a sale, going door to door, or throwing an advertisement on a billboard.

However, just because you can market a product a certain way doesn't mean you should. Allow me to teach you two of the most fundamental principles of marketing:

1. Marketing is not spamming. It is connecting a product with people who already want to buy that product (even if they don't know it yet). In some cases, it's finding the market first and developing the product to be perfect for that market (this is why we write to market).

2. In order to achieve the best marketing success, you must go where your audience is. Don't assume that if you build it they will come. Don't try to attract buyers, meet them where they already are.

Finding an existing audience, however, is easier said than done. There are many strategies that work for authors. But, in keeping with the 80/20 rule, I'm only going to touch on those that make the most sense for authors starting out, the ones that will grant you the most success with the least effort, meaning you can maximize your results. Generally, most of the effective marketing tactics fall into one of three buckets:

- **Advertising:** this is where you pay to play, i.e. spend money to get exposure. It's one of the most reliable forms of getting traffic, but often difficult because it costs money, therefore your conversion needs to be really good.

- **Content Marketing:** instead of spending money, content marketing requires that you spend time. This includes various platforms out there like YouTube, writing SEO articles, posting shorts on TikTok, etc.

- **Influencer Marketing:** Sometimes you can get others to promote your book for you. Newsletter swaps and group promotions are already a form of these, but they're not the only way to get other people talking.

There is a lot that could be said about all of these, but most of them are topics that deserve their own books, so I'm only going to cover some of the forms of marketing that are most effective for the cheapest cost (since you're just starting out. These techniques include the following:

- Newsletter swaps and group promotions (which we covered in step 2)

- Professional Book Promotions

- Advertising (maybe)

Content marketing, though one of the most powerful forms of marketing, is not something I'm going to cover here. That's mostly because it would require a whole section of its own. I think that most authors don't need to worry about it just yet, unless you want to build your audience through content marketing first, and then write your book later, which some people do.

I'll also briefly cover social media, and why I don't think it's the most effective use of your time.

The point with this section is to identify the easiest forms of marketing to work on first, and then we can branch out into more time/money intensive forms of marketing. But you're not there yet, you're just starting out as a writer, so let's start with the basics...

21

Book Promotions

We've talked about newsletter swaps before, which are free, but they are pretty much the only marketing strategy (besides social media and the ever-coveted word of mouth) that is free for you. Most other strategies will cost money. I'll have a chapter talking about how to budget these things, as this can sometimes be a major obstacle for authors who have no money starting out. But just know, this is an industry that (to a certain extent) is pay to play. There are some free and less-expensive options out there, but a proper book launch will almost never be completely without cost.

Book promotions are one such paid marketing strategy. What are book promotions? Simply put, book promotions are sites or services that will send out your book to their newsletters for money.

But wait? Didn't I say in a previous chapter that you should avoid spending money for newsletter shares? Yes, I did. But this is a different situation. You should definitely not pay for newsletter swaps. But in this case, these are newsletters devoted entirely to providing their readers with a list of books that are free or heavily discounted. That means, your book needs to be on sale to use them, usually free or $.99. Then, in exchange for your money, they will share the book, along with several others, to their email list.

BookBub is the king of these newsletters. None of the others even come close. They have literally millions of readers who use their service and hundreds of thousands for each major genre. The downside to BookBub is that it is almost impossible to get in, especially if you're exclusive to Amazon. You might try submitting your book a hundred times, and it's unlikely that you will ever get accepted. This is especially true when your book is brand new and doesn't have a lot of reviews or other social proof. BookBub does have a new releases newsletter, which you should definitely try when you're just starting. As always, it's worth trying. Thankfully, BookBub lets you submit your book to them every 90 days, and I strongly recommend you make a habit of doing this.

There are, however, plenty of other newsletters that do the same thing as BookBub (though with far less dramatic results). The good news is that these newsletters are usually quite a bit cheaper as well. The bad news is that they might not always make their money back. There are a few good ones, including the following:

- FreeBooksy (your book must be free when doing this promotion)

- Robin Reads

- Fussy Librarian

- BargainBooksy

- Book Barbarian (for Sci-fi/Fantasy)

- Red Roses Romance (for Romance)

- Book Adrenaline (for Thrillers/Mystery)

Now, there are a number of authors who will say that these book promotional sites no longer work. And it's true that they are no longer nearly as effective as they used to be. But, in my estimation, they are still one of the best ways to keep your book alive over time. Every few months, consider dropping the first book in your series down to $0 or $.99 and run a promotion or two on it. This will keep a semi-steady influx of new readers discovering your book.

However, there are a few downsides that I would caution you of. When it comes to book launches, some book promotions can be good, particularly those who section off their newsletters to the right audience. The problem is, none of that targeting gets very specific. For example, if I'm releasing a fantasy book, I can submit it to BookBarbarian, which specializes in science fiction and fantasy books. The problem is, I may want specifically YA Fantasy readers, or Arthurian fantasy readers. If I want Amazon to pick up my book and promote it to the right readers, I must ensure that my launch is targeting very specific readerships. BookBarbarian will be sending out my book to ALL science fiction and fantasy readers, which may be a little too broad.

And that is why I usually recommend book promotions as a way of keeping up steady sales every few months, and helping new readers discover you. It is one of many different avenues to do so, and can be very effective if used correctly.

That being said, there are many authors who have used strategically placed book promotions to great success. For instance, you can stack them over time in order to get that slow curve we talked about in a previous chapter. Say you start with one promotion, then the next day you do two, then three the next day, etc. Chances are, you could have some incredible growth this way.

But remember this does cost money, and if you do it well, there is another way to spend that money in a way that targets very specific readers...

22

ADVERTISING

Advertising is perhaps the most frustrating for authors, but if done right, can also be the #1 best way to get the readers you're looking for. In today's information age, it is entirely possible to target very specific subsets of people, finding exactly the type of person who would want to buy your book, and who actively reads in the niche genre you might be trying to reach.

Advertising can get really expensive really quickly, which is why it's often a source of great anxiety for many authors. And to be honest, it's probably one of the most expensive forms of marketing per individual sale even when done well, though some book promotions aren't much better.

Note that at first glance, your advertising might not look like it's being effective. In fact, in most cases you're unlikely to make back your advertising budget on just one book alone. This again emphasizes the need to have a series so that once people buy the other books in that series, you will eventually make back those monies you spent on advertising. But if your book is enrolled in Kindle Unlimited, you also have to factor that in. KU borrows count as sales in Amazon's eyes, but you won't see them reported, so it's impossible to know how many people borrowed the book if they're in KU. You'll be able to make an educated guess when you see how many KU page reads you have, but that's still not entirely accurate. Additionally, if you make a lot of sales through advertising, even if you spend more than you're making, it could be enough to trigger Amazon's algorithm so they begin to market your book for you. So there are a lot of different ways to measure the effectiveness of an ad, and not all of them will translate to direct sales.

I've mentioned it several times, but I must bring it up again: the importance of your book cover and blurb. These are the most essential tools in your advertising kit, because they are ultimately what people are going to see. Even if you have the best advertising campaign ever, once people arrive at your Amazon book page and see a crappy cover, you won't make any sales.

There are typically three main areas where authors spend their advertising money: Amazon Ads, Facebook Ads, and BookBub Ads.

This book is not meant to be an in-depth analysis of each individual platform, there are already some amazing books on the subject. In fact, here are some of those:

- **For Facebook:** Help! My Facebook Ads Suck, by Mal Cooper

- **For Amazon Ads:** Self-publishing with Amazon Ads, by Bryan Cohen

- **For BookBub Ads:** BookBub Ads Expert, by David Gaughran

What I will get into is the strength and weaknesses of each one, and how you might want to use them together. Just because there are three of them, doesn't necessarily mean that you should use all or one. If you understand the inherent value of each one, you will begin to see how you can use all three together, or maybe your particular marketing needs only require one. Whatever it is, it's important to know what sets each platform apart. But before we dive headlong into that, first I must introduce you to:

The Rule of Seven

I've heard variations of this rule, some say it's a rule of six, but most will say seven. The Rule of Seven states that a prospective customer will need to hear your marketing message at least seven times on average before listening to it. In other words, you need to advertise to a person at least seven times before you can reasonably expect them to buy your book.

Now the good news is that we've already tackled several ways in which you can get your voice heard. Your newsletter is one, and getting your book promoted in other author newsletters is another. But the best way to get exposure for your book so people are seeing it enough times is to use advertising.

Facebook Ads

Facebook ads have one advantage that some might also look at as a disadvantage: they spend all your money. I usually see this as a good thing, because it allows you to properly set a budget and pace yourself, and it keeps things expected. You know exactly how much you're spending, because you're in complete control of that number.

But, just because FB ads spend all your money, that does not necessarily make them effective. While Facebook is predictable, it can also be extremely easy to waste a lot of money on their platform. It requires constant supervision, and attention to detail (for example, you don't want to accidentally add a zero to your budget, or you could end up paying ten times what you had planned in a day. Believe me, it's happened).

Facebook charges you based on impressions, meaning the number of eyeballs that actually see your ad. Your job is to try and get as many clicks for those impressions as possible.

Side note: some impressions are more expensive than others, which means there may be multiple advertisers competing for those impressions. For that reason, you may want to stick with more niche targeting. Don't target Star Wars fans, for example and expect the impressions to be cheap.

One of the other nice things about Facebook is their targeting system. You can get super specific with the type of people you target. Generally speaking, one of the best ways to target on Facebook is to set up an audience of people who like specific authors in your genre. Then you narrow that down even further to people who like Amazon Kindle (or, if you're books are in more than one vendor, narrow it down by those vendors as well). You can also narrow based on country, language, age range, gender, and more. This is extremely useful in getting the most bang for your buck.

Now, as I mentioned above, it's your job to get as many clicks for the number of impressions you pay for. The more clicks you get, the lower your cost per result. We call this Cost Per Click, or CPC. I will talk more about how to get a low CPC at the end of this chapter when I talk about universal advertising tips for authors.

Amazon Ads

Amazon Ads have one big advantage over all the other ad platforms: your customers are already on Amazon, which means they're ready to buy. Amazon ads also charge you for clicks you receive, and not impressions. That said, Amazon Ads are growing increasingly expensive, since a lot of traditional publishers tend to dump a lot of money into their books.

However, there's one small reason why you might still want Amazon Ads in your strategy, even if you appear to be losing money: exposure. Amazon Ads can get your book in front of a lot of people. Remember the Rule of Seven? Well Amazon Ads are a great way for that to happen.

Amazon ads are probably where I would start (I used to say Facebook, but their ads have gotten consistently less effective). And again, the strategy that you will use will likely change over time as their algorithm changes, but given the placement of Amazon Ads, and that they've essentially switched to a pay-to-play model, it's almost essential to be running at least a small trickle of Amazon ads to see some results.

The good news is, if a trickle is working for you, you can scale a little more, then a little more, until you are successful.

BookBub Ads

BookBub Ads also have the advantage that they are very hyper-targeted at readers. The biggest problem with these readers, however, is that they're deal-seekers, which means they're unlikely to buy your book unless it's really discounted. That, combined with the fact BookBub ads can get very expensive, means that it's often very hard to make a profit on BookBub. Only a handful of people have been able to crack them, such as David Gaughran, which is why I highly recommend his book, *BookBub Ads Expert.*

But does that mean that you should just ignore BookBub ads entirely? Not at all. BookBub ads have their strengths, the biggest of these is the fact that BookBub ads are better at targeting the right kind of readers than almost any other platform. First of all, everyone who sees your ad is already a rabid reader. We know this because of the massive following that BookBub has. But BookBub is more than just an email list that sends out cool deals on books, it's also turning into a social network of sorts, much like Goodreads. Users can identify authors they like, and you can then target fans of those authors when you're crafting your ads.

Let's assume you have a book launch coming, perhaps even your first book. BookBub is a great advertising platform for book launches. Even if you lose money on BookBub ads, the kind of targeting you achieve will make it much more likely that you will properly train Amazon's algorithm to deliver your book to the right people. Sometimes, getting Amazon's algorithm to work for you is one of the best strategies for which you can use advertising. Yes, you should always try to get your costs down so that the sale of your books through that ad platform is paying for the cost of your ads alone. But when you're launching a series for the first time, that could be a secondary strategy to just getting plenty of sales from the right type of buyer. It will pay out in the end.

That said, BookBub is an ad platform where you should really try to know what you're doing before you throw a bunch of money at it. More than either Facebook or Amazon Ads, it is extremely easy to lose money in a hurry on BookBub ads. Don't just set a budget and forget about it. You must keep a close eye on these ads, or they will bleed you dry with few results to make up for it.

This is why I mentioned in a previous chapter that you should have some kind of short story or novella to experiment with before you launch your first proper series. Book-Bub ads will likely feel overwhelming if you just start playing with them right at your launch. You need to learn how to navigate them before that happens, just so you have a sense of what works and what doesn't for you. Reading David's book is another way to help understand these ads before you do anything too expensive.

But if you can get your costs down to a reasonable level, BookBub ads can still be a great help, especially when launching a new series. Typically speaking, when you launch a book, you'll usually have it discounted, which is what BookBub users love to see. Use them effectively, and you could soon have an avalanche of sales coming your way.

Universal Advertising Tips

Okay, now we get to the universal advice, regardless of what platform you're using. I place these last because they're incredibly important, and will likely continue to be important even when these ad platforms cease to be reliable. The ad market is constantly shifting, and what works now will likely not work even a few months from now. But these next tips are some that will continue to be important as long as advertising is a thing. The first, and most important of these tips is:

Test

There is not a single ad platform that I've mentioned so far, where testing is not the most important strategy that you must undertake. Thankfully, most platforms make this super easy. On Facebook, you can take the audience that you've set up, create several ads, then make sure each of them is exactly the same except for one single element: the picture. Then you simply sit back and watch carefully as each of those ads perform. You'll begin to notice that some ads are doing better than others, likely due to the picture you used.

Eventually, you can take the top two or three best-performing ads and copy them several times, this time using different wording for each. Since they all have the same photos, you should be able to tell from the difference in performance which text works best. If you keep repeating this process of duplication and then changing one tiny thing, you should eventually have an ad that is high performing in all aspects: the photo, the copy, everything. It's a constant process, but one that will only grow more profitable for you as time goes on.

This same process is also a really great way to handle BookBub ads. In fact, if you read any of the books I've recommended on advertising, you will see that their primary strategy for improving any ad is to experiment and try different things.

Stock Photo vs. Book Cover

With the exception of Amazon Ads, most ad platforms will allow you to use whatever image you want, as long as it doesn't violate any particular terms of use (you know what kind of images I mean). Facebook has some additional rules or recommendations that they enforce by forcing your ad to perform worse when you violate them, such as having too much text in your ad. Facebook wants the text to be the body of the ad, not in the image. BookBub has no such problems. They'll let you do just about whatever you want in your image (within reason) since there is no other place to put text.

Mal Cooper talks in her book *Help! My Facebook Ads Suck* about the best kind of images to use in your ads. The general consensus in that book is that stock photos work the best. I have found this to be true...for my CPC. Generally speaking, when I use a stock photo, I get more clicks, and therefore more bang for my buck. So naturally, you want to go with a stock photo, right?

Well, it's not actually that simple. David Gaughran in his book on BookBub ads says quite the opposite.

Oh, he admits that stock photos usually get more clicks. But when it comes right down to it, are clicks really what we want? Or do we want sales? David points out that in his experience, stock photos may get more clicks, but they won't convert as well. I've found that stock photos usually get me about one buy for every thirty clicks. Depending on how your book is priced, that can add up to be a lot of money with little return. David argues that a photo with your cover on it will sell better, even if it doesn't get as many clicks.

The logic behind this is that when people click on a stock photo, they might not realize that they're clicking on a book ad. This is particularly true of Facebook. But if people see a book cover, or art from a book cover, they'll know it's a book they're clicking on. That means that every click you get is specifically interested in that book. No wonder David insists that these clicks convert better.

I have personally tested out these two theories, and I believe David is correct that book covers sell a bit better. But they definitely do not get as many clicks, and maybe that's okay. Personally, I recommend doing a bit of both. There may be some readers who will only click on your ad because they like the stock photo, or there may be people who wouldn't buy your book unless they see a picture of it first. The results differ, and you don't want to put all your eggs in one basket.

As with anything related to advertising...test, test, test before you make any assumptions.

23

SOCIAL MEDIA

We've talked about Newsletter Swaps, Book Promotions, and Advertising, each of which I believe to be somewhat essential to getting great sales. They definitely fall under the 80% results that come from 20% of the work. But social media is a bit different.

Social Media and I have a bit of a love/hate relationship. Part of that is due to the fact that I believe social media is on the verge of a lot of change, given the fact that A) A lot of younger people are turning to other social-like networks that don't include heavy hitters like Facebook, B) There's been a lot of unrest among lawmakers and voters concerning privacy issues brought up by social media, and C) innovation in the tech world simply happens a lot, and we're due for some disruption.

But despite all of that, social media is still one well-used method of marketing your book. It's one of those elephants in the room that I simply have to talk about, even if I believe your efforts are best spent in more effective methods of marketing. At the very least, it can serve as a good platform for you to interact with your fans, and for your fans to interact with each other as well. That last part is something you can't get from other marketing avenues at the moment, outside of a forum on your website which readers are unlikely to use.

Social media is generally valued because you don't *have* to spend money on it. And yet, social media can be rather difficult to gain any headway without paying a lot of money. Also, there are just a lot of platforms, and they all work slightly differently, which means you need a different strategy for each one. That is why, in general, it's good advice to only pick one or two social media platforms and stick with those.

For most authors, I would recommend Facebook. Even though many younger people are not using Facebook, it's still one of the most widely used platforms, and one of the easiest to attract followers. And let's face it, young people don't have a ton of money for books. Your buyers are older and still on Facebook.

Instagram is another one that is often good for authors, as it's a great place to show pictures of your space, pictures of your book collection, and of course, your covers.

As a matter of fact, one of the best trending forms of social media marketing that is working really well right now is short form video. The nice thing about shorts is that you can use the same video in a variety of different social platforms, to maximize your reach. The big platforms right now are

Instagram reels (which can also go on Facebook), YouTube shorts, and of course, TikTok. If I could pick one form of social media marketing, this is what it would likely be.

But back to Facebook. As an author, you should probably set up an author page. Facebook groups are also highly useful. Anyone in your group is far more likely to see your posts than they would if they simply liked a page.

People on social media usually don't like it when you spam their feed asking them to buy your book. In all honesty, that's what Facebook ads are for. When you're interacting on social media, you should avoid actually goading people into buying your book. As you interact with people and make friends, over time people will get to know you, and that could lead to some sales. But for the most part, social media is simply an opportunity to interact directly with fans of your work, fans of the genre, and to allow those fans to interact with you, the author.

I'm not saying that you should avoid social media. Even though it does not lead to a lot of direct sales, it's still important for other reasons. But, if you're being worked to the bone by all the other things I recommend doing, and sales is your #1 goal, then it's okay to wait on this one. But eventually, you will want to revisit it, as it's important for authors to have a platform where readers can find them.

24

What to Do When You Have No Money

When I first started this book, it was my intention to try and structure it so it focused only on the things you can do for little or no money. Because first-time authors often have none. It's easy for an established author to throw thousands of dollars at advertising, because they've already made that money from past books, and they're likely to make it back again.

But what about you? Perhaps you don't have much money to spare. Perhaps book writing is your desperate hope for a plentiful life that you've never seen before. Perhaps you just lost your job and are looking for ways to make up for that loss.

Well, I've got some good news and some bad news. The good news is that it's still very possible to make a living as an author, and there are plenty of free or low-cost ways to make that happen.

The bad news is that it rarely does happen without first investing either money or a lot of time into your books.

I'm really sorry to say this, because I truly wish that there were easy ways around it, that you could just write that dream that's in your mind and start watching as the cash flows in. But it rarely works that way. If it did, everyone would be doing it.

And in fact, writing books is actually one of the least efficient ways to make money online, so if money is your goal, I would look elsewhere.

But most authors don't get into it for the money, although it is a necessity if said authors want to do it for a living, so money is usually a big goal.

When you're just starting out, you can budget yourself. Start well ahead of time to save up money for a good cover, and continue saving so you have a good advertising budget for your launch. Pace yourself and don't be impatient to get your book out there. It can wait a few months while you save up what you can. You can use this time to focus on certain other aspects of book marketing, such as building up your newsletter with your reader magnet and producing social media shorts.

Of all the things to spend money on, your book cover is the most important. If you can only afford to spend a couple hundred dollars on your book as a whole, make it your cover.

Now as I mentioned in the chapter on book covers, paying more doesn't necessarily mean your book cover will be better. A lot depends on the artist. And there's a common misunderstanding that books with custom illustrations (that an artist has to draw from scratch, and which cost a lot more) perform better than covers made from compositing stock photos and elements. In my experience, the stock-assembled covers perform just as well, if not better. Now, there are some genres where a good illustration will go a bit farther, such as epic fantasy. But even then, some of the best-performing fantasy I've seen uses stock elements. And it's much cheaper to go that route. If you're an author writing a genre with more generic-looking trends, such as romance or thrillers, then you can get your book covers for WAY cheap.

Buy pre-made covers, or do a search on Facebook for book cover artists that clearly do good work but don't have a lot of followers yet. These will be some of your best resources to getting good covers at a cheap price. Remember, your book cover does not have to depict a scene from your book or anything like that. It simply has to represent the tone of the genre.

Newsletter swaps are your other major tool if you're doing this with a low budget. They are still the only free way to get a significant amount of sales. Use your reader magnet long before your launch to try and build up a following on your newsletter, using an inexpensive service like StoryOrigin or Bookfunnel, then leverage that list in order to get other people to share your book when it's ready to launch.

And then, of course, there is social media. As I mentioned, it's not the most effective form of marketing, but it's also free. If you learn to navigate social media like a pro, you can still get a lot of good results out of it for no money at all. Just know that it will take a lot of time, and you can't just run into Facebook groups yelling about buying your book or you will get banned faster than you can say self-promotion. As I mentioned in the last chapter, if I were to focus hard on social media marketing, I would do so with short video content.

Here is a list of all the things that either won't cost you a cent, or are extremely important to use even if they cost money. I've tried to place them by order of what you need first, but they are all important. If they make this list, that basically means they're essential.

1. Writing the actual book

2. Your book cover (paid, but by far the most important thing to spend money on)

3. Your blurb (write it yourself using other blurbs as a model)

4. A proofreader (another one that costs, but not one you want to skip)

5. Newsletter (with MailerLite, free up to 1000 subscribers)

6. Writing a reader magnet for said newsletter

7. Newsletter Swaps (possibly the most important free marketing tactic on this list)

8. Social Media (if you have no money, go crazy on social media!)

So for those of you who have little to spare, this is where I'd start. In a way, this might be a good thing. Most authors did not start out with amazing returns on their first series. It's usually the second or third series that began to make them proper money. So perhaps it's good that you don't have a lot of money to start with, as you might then sink it into your first series and it wouldn't be that effective. By the time you get to your second or third series, that might be a better time to start really thinking about investing some mega-bucks into your projects.

Quick-fire Advise

Obviously, it's impossible to talk about everything that I would like to talk about in one little book this size. I do have more books for authors in mind, but my goal with this book was to cover what I consider to be the most essential advice for beginning authors. I believe I've done that so far, at least as far as the advice that I wish I had understood better when I was just starting out.

But there's still quite a bit of information we haven't covered, some of which is still very helpful. So, I'm going to try and cover each in a paragraph or two with my advice on how to deal with them, speed dating style.

Stick to one genre for now

When you're just starting out, you should try not to hop around to a bunch of different genres. Your readers will not follow you from one to the other. Stick to one specific genre for your first couple of series, then you can begin branching out after that.

If you're like me, then you can move in a strategic direction with your genres, slowly changing them so that there's more carryover from your readers. I started with YA Fantasy, but my plan is to move into more adult-level epic fantasy, which will presumably bring a lot of readers over from the YA crowd, but also allow me to build up a larger audience of epic fantasy readers, many of which are men. Then once I have that down as a solid audience, I'll start moving into space opera, which is still a lot like epic fantasy but in space. A lot of the men who read epic fantasy also read space opera, so hopefully I'll take some of those readers with me. But overall, expect to have to start from scratch when building an audience for a new genre.

KU vs. Wide

Kindle Unlimited (KU) is a source of great revenue for a lot of authors. But it requires that your ebook remain exclusive to Amazon for a period of three months, which will renew every three months until you stop it. Being in KU will mean you can't put your ebook up for sale on Apple, Barnes & Noble, Kobo, etc. But a lot of people do much better with their books if they're in KU.

My advice would be to start in KU, to help you get that added bump in your sales, which will result in more sales overall. Then, as the selling power of your series wanes over the months and years that follow, you'll find that you're not getting as much revenue through KU for that series. That's when you might want to consider taking it out of KU and launching it on other platforms.

Also, bear in mind that your exclusivity is limited only to ebook. While it's not likely to gain a ton of sales, you can always list your paperbacks on Kobo, Barnes & Noble, etc. If you use Ingram Spark to produce your print books, this isn't too hard to set up.

Going Direct

The exception to the KU vs Wide rule is going direct, which means you are creating your own store and selling on it. Now, this is a tactic that is a little more advanced, and so I haven't really mentioned it in this book. I recommend it's not something you try until you have at least two series written, and in the mean time, you can spend time learning Amazon's algorithm and all of the other tactics in this book.

But that said, going direct and selling books from your own store can be a great way to make a lot of money with your books, because you control the environment, you get the emails of your buyers, and more. The downside is that it's a lot of work, and you'll have to invent entirely new skills with Facebook ads to make it work.

Audiobooks

This is another area that requires a lot of money in most cases, but one that we cannot ignore. The market for audiobooks is growing faster than any other book market, including print and ebooks. If you want to be at the forefront of that trend, you should try and produce audiobooks for your books.

The problem is audiobooks are notoriously expensive, and can range anywhere from $2000-5000 dollars for an average-sized book. However, you can take the route where you do a royalty share with narrators. That will mean less money for you, but you won't have to put up any funds to get it out there.

If you're really strapped for cash, you can try using AI to narrate your book and sell that (but it will mostly have to be sold direct) until you can afford to hire a proper narrator.

Reviews

My best advice is not to worry about reviews that much. As your book sells, you will naturally get some reviews. As you build a newsletter, you can ask some of them if they'd like to receive a free copy of your ebook in exchange for a review. This is super helpful for your first book, where you'll probably want to see at least double digits on your reviews before you really start pushing the marketing. It's true that reviews matter, but they're also hard to get a lot of without first getting a lot of sales. Seriously, sometimes it can be like pulling teeth.

And trust me, you can still get sales with low amounts of reviews. And I know authors who somehow managed to get three figures on their reviews but their sales still went down eventually. If it stresses you, don't sweat it. Focus on more important things.

Launch Strategy

Here's a basic run down of what I do for a launch, and what I would recommend doing as well.

- Firstly, finish the book, and maybe a second or third, as well as the reader magnet (3-6 months before launch)

- Put your first book up for preorder at full price (3 months before launch)

- Release your reader magnet and begin entering it in book promotions like those found on Bookfunnel (3 months before launch)

- Spend the next few months using your reader magnet to build subscribers, and collecting newsletter swaps for your book. You can have other authors share your preorder, or you can ask them to wait (I would wait) until your book is live. (3-0 months before launch)

- Send out the occasional excerpt from your book to your newsletter, and do a cover reveal. (3-0 months before launch)

- First week of launch: try to arrange for most of your newsletter swaps that fit your genre to happen at some point during this week.

- Day 1: Release your book, but do not promote it. Feel free to buy it though. Celebrate!

- Day 2: Reveal your book to your least engaged newsletter subscribers. Start with a small amount of advertising and begin testing different photos to see which ones work best.

- Day 3: Reveal your book to your medium engaged newsletter subscribers. Increase your advertising budget and continue testing.

- Day 4: Reveal your book to your most engaged newsletter subscribers. Increase your budget even more, and begin trimming out the ads that are not performing well, focusing more on those that are.

- Day 5-10: Continue increasing your ad budget. What that budget looks like overall is up to you. I sometimes spend as much as $1000 over those first

10 days, starting with $5 on Day 2, and doubling with each new day.

- Week 2-4: Arrange for all of your newsletter swaps that didn't go on the first week to happen here. These will likely be swaps with people that aren't specifically in your niche genre, but maybe more generically tied to your genre (for example, I might have just YA fantasy in my first week, but open it up to epic fantasy, urban fantasy, etc. during weeks 2-4). Also, if you're scheduling any book promotions, set them up during this time, and try to keep them evenly spaced.

- If you're doing a rapid release, release your second book no later than a month after the first. A week or two weeks is even better. Make sure the book is available for preorder when your first book comes out, and that it's connected to your first book via a series page.

What About Websites?

I haven't talked about websites, because they're not really tools for sales (unless you're into content marketing). But it's important that you have a platform ready. If you know enough about websites that it isn't too much of a hassle to set them up, then go for it before you launch. Otherwise, it's okay if this one waits until after your first series has been released.

However, if you don't have a website when your first series launches, then you should at least have a Facebook page. You need some place where people can find you, even if you're not super popular yet.

Wordpress is an easy platform to set up, and many web hosting services will have quick one-click installs available for you on their servers. Then I'd recommend themeforest .com to find a paid theme for your Wordpress site. Some of the themes on that marketplace are breathtaking, and well worth the extra money. But if you're tight on funds, a free Wordpress theme will do.

Pen names

While this really isn't something you absolutely *need* to know when you're just starting out, it's useful information to tuck into the back of your brain while you're making plans for the future.

Should you use different pen names?

The answer can go any number of ways, and this has to do with the many reasons why you would want a different pen name. If your name is super hard to pronounce for people who make up most of your audience, then you might want to try something different. And if you're a guy writing romance, or a woman writing hard science fiction, you might also consider a pen name that is either gender neutral or completely gender swapped. Because, sadly, there will always be just a touch of sexism in the way people see authors in relation to the genre they're writing.

But the real reason I would consider taking on a new pen name is if I was writing a new genre that is completely different from the one I'm currently writing. That way you won't "contaminate" the sales of one genre with readers of another, which can throw off the algorithm. There's no hard and fast rule for this, but I'd say you'd probably want a different pen name for each umbrella genre, the really broad ones like thriller, romance, fantasy/sci-fi, or non-fiction. If you write both science fiction and fantasy, some authors would suggest you have two different pen names for those too, one for fantasy and one science fiction. I'd say that's decent advice, though I will be breaking it for my own work for one simple reason: all my fantasy/sci-fi books will be in the same universe. But if I were switching to billionaire romance, I would definitely get a pen name.

Pen names are not only good for changing genres, but also changing other things, like the...how do I put this delicately...cleanliness of your book. Just because erotica and sweet romance are both technically part of the Romance umbrella genre, does not mean you should use one pen name for both. You will get A LOT of angry reviews from readers who expected one thing and got another.

Is This the Only Way?

So far, I've given you a lot of advice in this book. We've talked about almost the entire book-producing process, from before you write, to your launch strategy. There have been a number of times when I've stressed that certain things had to be done in order to have success. But are those suggestions really the only way you should do it?

The answer to that is, of course not! I hate rules as much as I love to dish them out (my kids are going to hate me). Rules are made to be broken, and I mean that. That is how innovation comes. One person tries something new, and it ends up blowing up. Soon everyone is trying that thing, and it becomes saturated until it doesn't work as well anymore. Then someone else will try something new and the whole process will start all over again. This is standard innovation at its best.

But. AND THIS IS A VERY BIG BUT! True innovation usually comes from people who are already so familiar with the system, that they could work it in their sleep. Yes, it's true that sometimes outsiders with no internal knowledge of an industry can sometimes see things that others who are too close to the industry can't. But this is, honestly, rare. For example, I'm not going to suddenly have a brilliant idea that will change the way cars are made because I know almost nothing about cars except that they go on roads and stuff.

What you need is a healthy dose of insider knowledge, whilst maintaining the ability to think out of the box, and look at the industry with a more bird's-eye view. Only then can you break the rules in such a way as to spark innovation.

In other words, in order to understand the spirit of the law, you must first become a slave to the letter of the law. Once you have stuck to the letter for long enough that you know it by heart, only then will you be able to see clear paths to experiment, make mistakes, and innovate. But only if you maintain a curious, open mind.

For that reason, I do recommend sticking to the advice in this book, at least for now. Read other books, and see what they say. Assimilate all the knowledge you can, and you'll begin to see where all of us overlap. Take that knowledge, the stuff you see popping up over and over again, and put that into practice. I can guarantee that it will help you launch your first book series better than you would have done otherwise. If it doesn't...well remember this is still your first launch, and Rome wasn't built in a day.

Stay patient. With time, you will slowly build up a following, and that vision of success that you have in your head, no matter what it is, will slowly come to fruition. Don't ever forget that vision. Let it be your constant companion, and I think you'll go places.

Have Fun!

Lastly, don't forget that you should absolutely be having fun! Writing is such an awesome job. It's an exhausting job at times, but it's also amazing. Literally, being a writer is just about the closest you will ever be in this life to becoming a god, creating universes and worlds that spring off the page and into the minds of readers everywhere. It's truly a marvelous endeavor.

If you're not having fun with all this, if the stress of trying to build a business gets to be too high, or you find yourself wishing that you could walk away from your computer and never go back, hang in there. Just because it is sometimes hard to write, does not mean that you were not meant to be a writer. All of us have bad days, or even bad months. You can get through it, and you will feel so gratified once you do.

Perhaps there is something out there that will fulfill you more than writing a book, I can't say that there isn't. And if there is something out there that you absolutely love more than writing, by all means pursue it. I want you to be as happy as it is possible for you to be. But before you make that call, I would ask that you humor me for a while, and finish the book. Just finish it. Don't decide that writing isn't for you until you're holding that novel in your hands, you can smell the fresh paper, and feel the weight of your accomplishment in your hands. If you can do that, and still tell me that writing isn't for you, then I will be satisfied.

But I'm betting that won't happen. Because, for me at least, there is no better feeling than the one I've just described (note: I am not a father yet. I may have to edit this paragraph after that happens some day).

Ultimately, writing is one of the most fulfilling projects I've ever undertaken. Seeing my characters come to life will always be a highlight of my day, even when the writing becomes unbearably difficult at times. It is always worth it.

I wish you the best of luck in your endeavors. If you have a moment, feel free to say hello to me over at my website MythBank.com, or in one of our Facebook groups.

Now go write.

About the Author

Jason is a writer of mythic fantasy books. His passion for mythology and history led to him developing the encyclopedic website, MythBank.com, which ties directly into his books based on mythology, Arthurian Legend, and more.

He's currently living the dream within walking distance of the North Carolina beaches with his wife and daughter.

When he's not writing, his favorite hobbies include hiking, reading, playing with his daughter, and developing his websites. See more of his books at MythHQ.com as well as some informational articles on Arthurian Legends and Mythology at MythBank.com.

The Site

www.mythhq.com

The Membership

https://mythbank.com/go/membership

Twitter

twitter.com/storyhobbit

Instagram

instagram.com/storyhobbit

TikTok

tiktok.com/@storyhobbit

Email

jason@mythhq.com

ALSO BY JASON HAMILTON

Roots of Creation

A New Light (short story)

Out of Shadow

Growing Ripples

Through Fire

Into Storm

To World's Above

As Winter Spawns

Seeds of Hope

In Creation's Heart

The Faerie Queen

Path of the Dragon

Lair of the Siren

Rage of the Beast

Strength of the Heroes

Fall of the Faerie

Rise of the Queen

Story Hacker Secrets

10,000 Words an Hour
From Zero to Published
The Plot Module